T0115091

JUSTICE FOR LORRAINE

CONRAD COHEN

abbott press®
A DIVISION OF WRITER'S DIGEST

Abbott Press books may be ordered through booksellers or by contacting:

Abbott Press
1663 Liberty Drive
Bloomington, IN 47403
www.abbottpress.com
Phone: 1-866-697-5310

Because of the dynamic nature of the Internet, any web addresses or links contained in this book may have changed since publication and may no longer be valid. The views expressed in this work are solely those of the author and do not necessarily reflect the views of the publisher, and the publisher hereby disclaims any responsibility for them.

Any people depicted in stock imagery provided by Thinkstock are models, and such images are being used for illustrative purposes only.
Certain stock imagery © Thinkstock.

ISBN: 978-1-4582-1417-1 (sc)
ISBN: 978-1-4582-1416-4 (hc)
ISBN: 978-1-4582-1415-7 (e)

Library of Congress Control Number: 2014902208

Printed in the United States of America.

Abbott Press rev. date: 4/9/2014

Why the Book?

December 31, 2012 was three years since the death of my wife from Aspiration Pneumonia at Little Forks Hospital. This was the result of 52.5 mg of the drug Zyprexa in five days from October 7 through October 11, 2009. Fifteen of the 52.5 mg given to her on October 11, 2009; 5 mg in the afternoon and overdosing her with 10 mg more in the evening. It was given to her by Dr. Dave Camel, our family doctor and helped by Marjorie Nelson PAC (Physician Assistant Certified) of Psychiatry at Crater Memorial Hospital. They also put a DNR (Do Not Resuscitate) order on her chart without consulting me. What did we (you and me) get out of this very important book?

I remember one night coming home from The Nursing Home of the Angel where I had to place my wife after Dr. Camel and Nelson, PAC finished with her. I stopped to see a good friend of mine, Dave, and he was eating shrimp and lobster sauce he had gotten from a Chinese take-out place nearby. I said I used to love that a long time ago. I'll get some when I leave and take it home and I did. At home I ate some and then prepared to go to bed. Then suddenly my face was itching and I looked in the mirror and my face was blotchy.

I called the pharmacist. After I told him what I ate, he told me I must be allergic to seafood and to come down right away. I got dressed and went down to see him. He said I better go to the Emergency Room at Crater Memorial Hospital. They took me as soon as they saw me and were preparing to give me an IV of Prednisone and were ready to put an ID tag on my wrist and I started to yell, "You're not going to admit me, my wife was killed by a doctor at this hospital and I'm not staying!." They called in a woman doctor and she said "Your throat will close and you will die." I said, "Promise me you won't admit me." She said, "I promise you as a doctor, I won't admit you." I said, "Promise me as a woman because I don't trust doctors. They kill here and I don't want to be killed like my wife." She promised as a woman and I let them give me the IV and put the ID on my wrist. I was remembering they put DNR on my wife's wrist without discussing it first with me for permission.

I was never so scared in my life and to this day, I don't trust or look up to doctors as I once did. One killed my wife and to me, the word "doctor" is just a synonym for horror.

The reason becomes clear why I wrote this book. I had to. I had to get my wife's story out. People have to know what could and does happen to their loved ones when they enter a hospital where it's the doctor's turf and he does what he wants.

I carry the horror of what they did to her in my mind. I know about every second what happened in that hospital because I found my answers in her medical records. After she was overdosed, everything became very clear to me what happened to my helpless wife, all done behind my back. If someone made a TV movie about it, only I could play me.

I want people to be safe in the hospitals and that's only possible when there is trust in those people with whom we leave our loved ones, like the doctors, nurses and other medical staff responsible for the safety of the patients. It is a serious national problem and those in the medical field have to be held accountable for any wrong doing on their part on helpless people. Yes, I certainly am thinking of a non-caring doctor.

Patients have rights. Families should open their mouths when there is something wrong happening to their loved ones. Take action. This is a wake-up call to those who bury their heads in the sand when something happens. Things have to change and people have to change. We have to take control of our lives as far as the medical profession is concerned. I wish there were hearings on the subject and I would go to the head of the line to testify about doctors and those who protect them. I've had firsthand experience for over three years and I have plenty to tell. Justice is one word neither the medical community nor those who regulate the medical community cares about. I DO! My wife was taken from me without cause by a doctor and his cohort, a PAC from Psychiatry. I'll never stop trying to get "Justice for Lorraine" and I'll love her and cherish her with my broken heart until the day I die.

Book Dedication

This book is dedicated to my darling wife Lorraine who was and still is more precious to me than all the gold in the entire world. She was the epitome of what men look for in a woman: beauty, intelligence, sense of humor, loving, caring, loyal, great dancer, to name a few of the fantastic qualities she had. We were crazy in love with each other for 38 years from the first time we looked at each other till the day she died. I've cried for her every day since.

I was holding her hand when the nurse came into the hospital room to take her vitals and I saw a little ooze from her eye near her nose and tried to get it out. She yelled "OH MY EYE." I kissed her and said I was sorry hon. That was the last words she spoke on earth. She had spoken a few words only three other times since Oct. 11, 2009. It was now Dec. 31, 2009 at 6 am. She died at 10:55 am Dec. 31, 2009, 2 ½ months since her overdose from Dr. Camel from Aspiration Pneumonia. I thank God for all the time I had her with me: Thirty-eight years.

Lorraine's courage is unparalleled anywhere. She had a strong will to live but it wasn't enough. The staff at the Nursing Home of the Angel were fighting along with her.

That's why I love them so much.

FOREWORD

This book could not have been written without the efforts of an amazing woman by the name of Ruth-Ann Goode. She is a brilliant therapist who operates like a forensic psychologist by using their techniques to help her client to become a whole person again after going through a tragic situation, She has the ability to recognize your inner talents and bring them out to optimum potential and you haven't a clue what she's doing. She's that good.

My wife died Dec, 31 2009 and I am thankful I chose her to get me well again. Since Jan 2010, I see her two times a week and look forward to every session. I was a victim of my wife's death by our own family doctor, spoken to five lawyers who refused to take the malpractice suit, closed out two times by the medical board to whom I made a complaint against the doctor to get justice for her. Now all of a sudden I'm telling our story of her death and the treatment I received. So somewhere in my inner being Ms Goode found a writer with one sentence to me.: "Why don't you write a book about how your wife was killed and what you were subjected to in pursuit of justice!" I owe everything to "the amazing one" and will forever be in her debt. Ruth-Ann is a very skilled person and knows an awful lot about a lot of things. I'm glad she's on my side. How do I know that? Because she has always been there for me, that's how! She is one in a million.

#2 Foreword

Another person in my life who is very important to me who richly deserves recognition for being a true friend, advisor, and confidante for close to twenty-five years is <u>Mariska Bornak</u>. Our relationship is one closer to that of step-father and step-daughter. She ran a doctor's office here in Cedar so is quite knowledgeable of the medical field. She has always been there for me and always with the right answers.

Mariska has relocated to another state and lives happily at her job as a gov't biller of the local hospital and tending her garden and traveling. We remain in close touch with each other and she is a fan of the reason for the book.

TO A VERY DEAR FRIEND

What I've got now is my confidence back and you helped me and I'll forever be grateful to you. You saw things I couldn't because I was blinded by the grief I felt. I'm not afraid any more. At different points you led me to where I am today. I am now a storage of information that is starting to flow in this book. A book like this is long overdue and badly needed for people to have faith again and not be afraid to face these doctors and take on the people who are protecting them. I am God's instrument to do it.

Remember, I told you that my Hebrew name is "Yisrael" which means "God's helper" and I'm going to expose the doctor and PAC who killed my wife at the hospital and those who protected them and prevented me from getting justice for my wife.

When I had my eco-cardiogram last year the nurse let me hear my blood rushing in my body and that's how I feel now only with words rushing through my brain eager to get it on paper.

BACKGROUND

Lorraine Hallow   Born December 4, 1933   Richmond, VA
                       Died December 31, 2009   Little Forks Hospital

Conrad Cohen   Born December 5, 1927   Brooklyn, NY

Lorraine was a beautiful blonde, blue eyed kid, adolescent and grown woman. Since she was tall, she played basketball in public school. She went to Thomas Jefferson High School in Richmond, VA. I'm not sure if she played basketball in high school, but she was into rock and roll, country music, dancing and traveling.

She was working for Ma Bell Telephone Company when I met her. Our meeting is covered in another chapter. I remember when I used to go to her hometown to visit her at Ma Bell. It looked like the old movies with telephone girls all lined up sitting in a row with telephones plugging in calls and the phones across the top of their heads. Remember this was in the 1960's (of course I didn't meet her until November 25, 1972) and Lorraine walked into work with long slacks, not the dresses they were all wearing and they all looked horrified. The supervisor, a male, came in to see what was wrong. When he saw her in slacks he became horrified too and immediately said to Lorraine "Take off those pants!" So Lorraine, always the rebel, dropped her pants and the supervisor again screamed and Lorraine replied, "Well, you told me to take them off!" She then pulled her pants up and went to put on a dress. She was labeled a rebel and afraid of no one. When Ma Bell was short of repairmen, she even climbed poles, in workpants, naturally.

I came to Richmond to pick her up and take her with me to Century Park, PA. She quit Ma Bell, I started teaching college and our life together began. She confided in me about the abuse she, her mother and brother suffered at the hands of her drunken father. I swore to her that she would never have a bad day in her life from that day on. I kept my promise and gave her a beautiful life, just as she gave me. When the doctor gave her Zyprexa, that wound up killing her, it broke the string of being in love and happy.

I, on the other hand, after public school, went to Abraham Lincoln High School in Coney Island, Brooklyn. Up to that time, I played in the streets the games such as, stick ball, punch ball, kick the can, ring-a-levio, Johnny on the Pony, skelly, marbles, flipping baseball cards, box ball, to name a few. I played baseball for Lincoln High and after graduating in June 1945, I enlisted in the U.S. Navy at the age of 17 ½. I was sworn in on July 28, 1945. the war in Europe was over, but not with Japan. Later, my ship was part of the atomic bomb testing at Bikini Atoll in the Pacific. I also played baseball for my ship. When I was discharged on December 4, 1948, I worked at various jobs. After that I took the exam for police officer with the New York City Police Department. I made it and was sworn in on October 1, 1952. I met Lorraine on November 25, 1972 (covered in another chapter), retired in April 1973 and took a teaching position with Century Park University of Pennsylvania.

How We Met and Our Life Since November 25, 1972

The magic number to the start of a happy life with the most beautiful girl in recorded history.

It was November 25, 1972. I was a police officer with the New York City Police Department and just finishing an 8:00 a.m. to 4:00 p.m. tour and heading for the Piccadilly Hotel on West 45th Street between Broadway and 8th Avenue, which I frequented when off duty. I walked into the bar off the street and saw this beauty sitting at the bar. I came in and our eyes met and as Humphrey Bogart said to Claude Raines at the close of the movie "Casablanca" when they walked into the fog at the airport, "Louie, I think this is the beginning of a beautiful friendship!" We both had one heart and knew we had to be with each other the rest of our lives and then through eternity afterwards. I was there to meet some friends. She was there on a vacation from Richmond, VA where she lived and worked. That exact moment in time we became one heart and one soul. One and a half years later, on August 29, 1974, we were married and had the most wonderful life for almost 38 years, until her death on December 31, 2009. Our official date of marriage was August 29, 1974, but we always believed we were married under God's eye on that very first day we met on November 25, 1972

Lorraine's birthday was on December 4th and mine was on December 5th, so during those first dates in 1972 we went ice skating at Rockefeller Center and had a great time falling over each other. She was of the Methodist denomination and I was Jewish. In the Jewish faith we light memorial candles on the date of our loved one's death according to the Jewish calendar. I light candles according to the Gregorian calendar and the Jewish calendar. Religion never came between us. We loved each other dearly and we became each other's priority.

We went to a campground in Walden, North Carolina to visit her parents on August 29, 1974. We decided to marry and went to town to City Hall and we made arrangements. Lorraine and I then went to a judge living in town and he asked if we had two witnesses. We said "no" so he said to wait one minute and went to the telephone. Shortly later, a police car pulled up; the two police officers got out and we now had our witnesses to the marriage. Fate being what it is, two brother cops were our witnesses and sent us from the judge's house as man and wife. And so our beautiful life began. We went back to the campgrounds and told her parents we were now married!

While with the police department, I went to John Jay College of Criminal Justice and got a Bachelor of Science in Police Science and a Master of Public Administration. I retired in January 1973 and accepted a position with Century Park University of Pennsylvania teaching criminal justice, then three years later transferred to Cedar State College.

Our life took an upward turn when I started teaching. At the college level, you get a lot of time off with long Christmas breaks, summers off, Spring breaks, etc. giving us lot of time to travel. We both loved to travel and together, we explored the world. Without sounding like a travel agent, we enjoyed places like Florence and Rome, Italy, Germany, Athens, the Greek Islands, Istanbul, Turkey, six weeks in Spain, Algeciras in Southern Spain and we crossed the Mediterranean Sea to the Casbah in Morocco. We sunned and honeymooned in Acapulco and, of course, every year on August 29th, we went to Niagara Falls, the "Honeymoon Capital" for everyone.

In 1986 we started cruising and took fifteen cruises everywhere in North, South, East and West Caribbean Sea through the Panama Canal, Alaska (our absolute favorite.) and the Mexican Riviera (Cancun, etc.). To list all the places we visited would be a little much, but you get the idea. We were always on the go, enjoying the places and each other and taking care of one another. Our life was wonderful and I can truly say we never argued about anything; a rarity in marriage, but nevertheless, true for us.

When we left each other for any reason, we kissed and told each other, "I love you." When we met again we kissed and said, "I love you." When we went to bed, we kissed and said, "I love you." When we got up in the morning we kissed and said, "I love you." We had the warmth and tenderness always for each other. It truly was a match made in heaven. She could shimmy like Tina Turner and we loved to go dancing.

I retired from teaching after 25 years in August 1997. We then had a set-back after making possible plans to leave Pennsylvania. My dear wife had a stroke after a successful operation on her colon.

She was in the ICU in Roper City Hospital and I arranged to have her admitted to Sacred Lamb in Morganville PA. She was there a month, did very well in her recovery and then went to Lakeside Rehabilitation in Cedar. She went to Lakeside with a walker and was determined to rid herself of it. And she did! Insurance covered about a month and a half but they had a Post Discharge Program. We paid $20 a month and were able to use the facility as long as the place was open and stay as long as we wanted. We went three times a week, worked on all the physical equipment and signed up for speech therapy. We set an all-time record of going there for five years. She was great on all the machines; treadmills, lifting weights, leg exercises, bicycle. Lorraine did so well. One day I suggested we take the day off and she naturally answered, "No, we'll take a day off when I can walk as well as I used to." She was a marvel to watch and I was so proud of her or I should say even prouder than ever before.

1. This will include areas we traveled to that were inadvertently left out when I discussed our travels. Some of the places we visited were:
   A. The Lost City of Atlantis which is located off the Island of Crete in the Mediterranean Sea which separates Greece and Turkey. Artifacts can be seen through the clear water off the island. The following four days we visited Athens, the Acropolis, the Greek Islands, the Parthenon and Istanbul, Turkey. While in Istanbul we visited the spectacular Hagias Sophia, once the largest church in Christendom.
   B. Super Bowl XVIII in Tampa, Fl. It was January 18, 1984 the Los Angeles Raiders were playing the Washington Redskins.

Lorraine and I were both Pittsburgh Steelers fans so naturally we rooted for the Redskins since the Raiders were rivals of our team. When the first half was over the Redskins were playing bad so we started rooting for the Raiders. The game ended Raiders over Redskins 18-9.

C. The Belmont Stakes in New York. This being the third part to the Triple Crown in horse Racing. The first part of the Triple Crown is the Kentucky Derby in Kentucky. Followed by Pamlico in Maryland and the final being the Belmont. We also enjoyed going to the races in Saratoga Springs in New York.

D. Lorraine and I both enjoyed the outdoors. A favorite summer trip we would do was whitewater rafting on the Colorado River in Durango, Colorado during the summer months.

Our Life Starts in Century Park, PA then onto Cedar, PA

After I retired in 1973 I took a position with Century Park University of Pennsylvania one of the twelve PA State colleges. I was an Assistant Professor and taught criminal justice courses in the Department of Criminology. Later I became Chairman and started a graduate program in Criminal Justice.

We lived in a brand new townhouse, one that was just built in a new complex with a balcony overlooking the beautiful countryside. It was like a country club with a large main building. This was owned by the VFW of which I was a member and the complex had a beautiful swimming pool, tennis courts and golf course. Our active life was about to start. We would swim, we played tennis, no golf, and joined a bowling club. Lorraine won two or three trophies. (Now the best part) The VFW had meals served in a delightful dining room twice a week at reasonable prices and dancing every Saturday night. We never missed the dancing. The music was not a nickelodeon but we danced to a live band! In the winter the VFW also had a tremendous fire place and soft leather chairs to warm up at the fireplace with a little brandy. Lorraine was into the arts and crafts and decorated everyone's sandals with jewelry and colored stones.

We missed the food of New York and drove often. At times I'd call my mother and she'd make us some good home cooking. We also went to New York to see a Broadway show or go to the opera.

James Stewart, the actor-cowboy, was born in Century Park, PA and his father had a hardware store on Main Street. People used to come to see their home. There was a centennial dinner at the college and Jimmy Stewart and his wife came. Everyone lined up to say hello to them at the dais. Lorraine was lucky; Mrs. Stewart took off her corsage and gave it to Lorraine.

For Christmas of 1974, I gave Lorraine a player piano and we got dozens of rolls to play. Our favorites were "Dueling Banjos" and "How Great Thou Art." Lorraine was tall and had beautiful thin legs and when she played Dueling Banjo her legs moved like lightening. When friends were invited to our house, they marveled at her energy and couldn't believe her powerful legs playing the songs. I couldn't believe how she moved those legs without getting tired.

Then things changed at the college and I talked it over with Lorraine. We decided to make a change and go east. A teaching job opened up at Cedar State College and I applied for it and got the position. It was treated as a transfer within the twelve college system so now we were closer to New York being on the border of New Jersey.

In Century Park, Pa, we used to go to honky tonks and dance. We wanted to find a place in or near Cedar where we could dance. We found one about thirty miles north in Johnson's Corners, PA. I had a Pennsylvania State Trooper in one of my classes who worked in the Johnson's Corners area and he had told me about Laurel Villa in Johnson's Corners, PA, a popular vacation resort, famous for its modern comforts and excellent cuisine. So we went up there once and absolutely loved it.

Saturday night became Laurel Villa night and the only time we didn't go was because of snow. We met the State trooper and his wife and soon became fast friends. They would come to our house and visit but not on Saturday nights. That was dance night. It became a joke with other dancers we met there because everyone knew Lorraine never wanted to stop dancing. Others would stop and rest. Lorraine and I had the dance floor to ourselves and I'd ask her if we could stop and rest and she would say, "No, when the band takes a break we will!"

We did this for about four or maybe five years, until Laurel Villa closed. We had a good run though.

We concentrated on our vacations from teaching and continued to travel and see anything we missed. It was easy living with a woman like Lorraine. So beautiful and kind and loved me like I loved her. I thank the Lord for that.

Hey Houlihan

It was in the early 1980s when we made an Amtrak trip from New York to New Orleans. The trip was an experimental one to see the value of changing the dining arrangements from the sit-down service to cafeteria style. All the top brass of Amtrak and the dining establishments were aboard and they had the dining car all fixed up for cafeteria style eating. Lorraine and I loved New Orleans so it was exciting for Amtrak to do the driving for us.

We used to drive everywhere. We didn't take a sleeping car; we sat in the lounge with plenty of room to throw our legs up and had a ball. Naturally, the train didn't miss a stop at every town or city on the way down.

The night before we got to New Orleans, we stopped for the night at a honky-tonk town outside New Orleans. Just about everyone aboard left the train and went to a club called Houlihan's. It looked like a movie theater with tables and chairs where you could sit and eat. The stage had room for a band and plenty of space for dancing. Lorraine and I, together with friends we made on the train, ate, danced and had a great time. Then the dance floor emptied and it suddenly became amateur night. People were performing solos, singing or dancing. The band stayed on the stage to accompany the soloists. Then, who goes up but my baby Lorraine. She was not afraid or shy when it came to dancing. She did her world famous shimmying and the band played "The River," Tina Turner's noted and famous song. Lorraine tore down the house with everybody yelling "Go Tina" and "Go Houlihan." She had endless energy and I joined the screamers yelling "Go Baby, Go Baby!" I got up on the side of the stage yelling proudly, "She's mine! She's mine and I'm hers!" Everybody was screaming back "She's ours!" Then Lorraine said to the band, "I have to go to the bathroom, I'll be right back" and she left the stage. The funniest part was some others went on the stage to sing or dance and the crowd booed them off and were screaming, "we want Houlihan."' Lorraine came back shortly and started again and this time she told the band she wanted to dance to rock and roll music and then country-western, her favorite music. Naturally my favorite was the Big Band. And After a while, it all ended because it was very late and we had to go back to the train.

The next morning when Lorraine and I went to the cafeteria-style dining car, the staff greeted us with "Hey Houlihan!" They had been there too. What a glorious evening we had. For quite a while afterwards, I called her "Hey Houlihan."

The next day we reached New Orleans. The train stayed there a few more days so we were able to fully enjoy New Orleans. I never knew if the cafeteria-style eating aboard Amtrak ever made it, but we never forgot Houlihan's. Years later we would still talk about it and laugh. We were so happy and so in love.

CRUISING

I mentioned earlier that we loved to travel and we loved Acapulco, Mexico. We loved Acapulco so much that we spent our honeymoon there at the Hotel Las Brisas in January 1975, after our marriage on August 29, 1974. Las Brisas is the most beautiful place in the world. It's on a mountain and each room has its own private outdoor pool. Every morning breakfast is left at your door in a basket. The rolls were always so fresh. You had your own Jeep at your disposal should you want to go to town. You could also drive to the cliffs and watch the divers, watch the parasailors in the air, or just drive around the beautiful Acapulco Bay. We both went parasailing and we were thrilled by the experience. The warm nights were ideal for the delicious meals at dinnertime and the band provided Grand Mexican Music for dancing and we danced all night. It was paradise to be at such a locale with someone like Lorraine to love and be loved in return. I thank God for the years he had given us. We didn't waste any of the time given to us.

We travelled all over the World but our love remained constant. Acapulco was like our home base for January. We would stay at the Acapulco Plaza for a week or ten days. We would buy some clothes there made by a local tailor and eat at Carlos & Charlie's, a famous local eatery, then get plenty of sun. We were sun-worshippers from our early days. As children, we loved the beach, Lorraine in Virginia Beach, Virginia and I at Coney Island, Brooklyn, New York.

As long as we were together we could go anywhere and it was like our Honeymoon. It was uncanny how our love was so strong. We just wanted to be together and we were together.

A strange thing happened in 1986, after all these years in Acapulco, Acapulco changed. They started catering to the younger people who flocked there on Spring Break. It turned us off. So, in 1986 was our last year there and it turned us to cruising.

Our first cruise was January 3 - 10, 1987. We spent seven days on the Cunard Countess – "Caribbean Capitals Tour" and we went to San Juan, Puerto Rico to Caracas, Venezuela, then Grenada, St. Georges to Barbados, Bridgetown to Martinique, and Fort De France to Saint Thomas, U.S. Virgin Islands and ended at San Juan.

I remember when I was still a police officer with the NYC Police Department and covered the West Side of Manhattan from West 42nd Street to West 59th Street. There were not any cruises leaving the Hudson River Boat Docks. There were transatlantic crossings and various countries would sail in and left from the Atlantic Ocean. The countries and their ships are as follows:

United States: United States
France: Ille De France
Germany: The Bremen
Italy: Leonardo Da Vince and Michelangelo

The Police Department has a special squad of Police Officers handling the crowds on the dock, but our job when ships came in and left with another load of people going back we had to park our radio car and handle the cars coming in to pick up arriving passengers. After all the people passed through customs, we were invited by the ship's captain to come aboard and eat. The dining room was prepared to serve meals and wine, just as they would be serving the passengers. The whole dining room was filled with all guests of the captain and special tables were set aside for the police department. We ate and drank as if we were dining when the ship was at sea. There were guests and guests of guests. It was the mid 1960's when Transatlantic crossings stopped and vacations cruising was born. Lorraine had taken some cruises with her girlfriends before we met, so she was ready for our "Cruising Era." The following page has our 15 cruises. Lorraine was friendly with a man who owned World Wide Cruises in Fort Lauderdale, Florida. She would call him and ask him if he had any good deals. The ship lines usually give the travel agents some cabins so they can give their regular customers a good deal for a better price. Lorraine did well for us. That travel agent sold out to American Express, but still took care of us.

As mentioned previously, Alaska was our all-time favorite cruise. We drove to Vancouver, Canada to pick up our ship. Lorraine didn't fly. Our first stop was Juneau, Alaska and lo and behold, we took a helicopter to get to the Mendenhall Glacier. She really enjoyed the ride. That was my dearest Lorraine. The trip was topped off by a right turn off route 80 at Des Moines, Iowa and we travelled 100 miles to Eldon Iowa. This is where Tom Arnold, "Roseanne's husband" has a diner. If you watched their television show, you will remember that they had a diner that served "loose meat" sandwiches. Roseanne wasn't there so we had two loose meat sandwiches. I had the Tom Arnold sandwich and Lorraine had the Roseanne sandwich. When the diner was pretty cleared, I went to the kitchen and met their chef, Bitsy, who gave me the recipe. When at home, I made the recipe, but I had a question, so I called the diner, spoke to Bitsy and got my question answered. We had a great cruise and went to the diner for lunch at our favorite TV program and personality, Roseanne. Even if we didn't see her there, we still had fun. There were plenty of pictures of them on the walls.

So there you are with cruising. You never know what and whom you will see, but know that there will be plenty of music to dance to on all cruises. Oh, did I tell you we loved to dance?

Our latest cruise was January 3 – 10, 2004. It was our fifteenth and final cruise, yes fifteen glorious cruises. We never took another cruise or went anywhere again except to doctors for Lorraine when she got sick. We went to Jefferson Hospital in Philadelphia, Geisinger in Danville, PA, Union Memorial Hospital in Baltimore, MD and Allentown, PA. She was diagnosed with dementia in 2005.

THIS TIME IT'S CRUISING FOR SURE

Cruise # 11 January 2nd – 16th, 2000 – 14 days

Holland-American Line "Nieu Amsterdam"

"Southern Caribbean": Tampa, FL, San Juan, Puerto Rico, St. John, US Virgin Island, St. Thomas, Pointe Pitre Guadalupe, Bridgetown, Barbados, Castries, St. Lucia, Isla Margarita, Venezuela, Bonaire, Aruba, Grand Cayman, Tampa Fl.

I chose this cruse to write about because southern people, like my wife from Richmond, Virginia, have traditions like having black-eye peas on New Year's Day for good luck and good fortune for the year. Since our cruise started right after New Year's Day, my wife brought three cans to share with our shipmates. We had this experience on other vacations, that's why we brought three cans. The ship got underway at 4:00PM on January 2nd and by January 3rd we were well underway. That day some chefs were cooking hamburger, fries, hot dogs and other goodies, poolside. My wife took out the cans of black-eyed peas and kindly asked the chef to warm them. Sometimes stewed tomatoes are added to the peas, but the tomatoes are optional. When the black-eyed peas were warming the aroma drifted over to the people on the food line. Then a separate line formed for the peas. Lorraine didn't mind sharing until one woman just stood there where the chefs were serving the peas and kept asking for more in her bowl. So my baby went there, closed the line and made the chef almost empty the screaming woman's bowl. Lorraine said that we brought the food on board and it was not the ship's food, and if you're going to eat like you're "going to the chair" then you're cut off from eating my food! Everyone on "Lorraine's line", including the woman who was misbehaving, ate normal portions and murmured to each other, who is that woman?" They said her southern accent didn't go with her actions. Lorraine overheard the comments and said, "I got that from my Yankee Husband. It worked, didn't it?" She was great!

Holland American line is noted for having real good food because they get their meat from Australia and New Zealand. The ports we hit each had something good and different. St. Lucia in the West Indies loaded with college students trying to make the grade when they couldn't in their own countries. The shopping in Bonaire and Aruba, are both known for quality clothes and goods at very affordable prices. I am now honoring my wife's tradition by eating black-eyed peas on New Year's Day. It will always be at home too, because forever I'll be a solitary animal without my mate. That's my choice.

(15 CRUISES)

1) Jan. 3-10, 1987 7 Days: "Cunard Countess" "Caribbean Capitals" - San Juan to Caracas,
    Grenada, Barbados, Martinique, St. Thomas; back to San Juan.

2) Jan. 16-23, 1988 7 Days: "Costa Riviera" Port Everglades, St. Thomas, St. Croix, Nassau

3) Jan 7-14, 1989 7 Days: "Carnival Holiday". Western Caribbean: Miami - Playa (Carmen);
    Cozumel, Grand Cayman, Ochos Rios

4) March 16-23, 1991 7 Days: "Commodore - Caribe I": Miami : Puerta Plata (Dom. Republic)
    San Juan, St. Thomas

5) Jan 5-12, 1992 7 Days: "Costa Marina": Miami - Cozumel, Ochos Rios, Grand Cayman

6) Jan 2-9, 1994 7 Days: "Holland Ame. Noordam" Eastern Carib. Port Everglades.
    Nassau, San Juan, St. Thomas.

7) May 22-29, 1994 7 Days "Princess - Golden": Alaska. Vancouver - Juneau,
    Skagway, Glacier Bay, Ketchikan

8) Jan 8-15, 1995 7 Days: "Costa Romantica" Eastern Carib: Miami - San Juan, St. Thom
    Dom. Republic (Serena (Cay, Casa de Campo)) Nassau

9) Jan 7-17, 1996 10 Days "Princess - Sky" Panama Canal - Port Everglade - Princess Cays,
    Limon, Costa Rica, Panama Canal, Cartagena, Colombia,
    Cozumel, Mex.

10) Jan 4-11, 1998 7 Days: "Norwegian Dreamward" - Western Carib. - Miami -
    Georgetown Grand Cayman, Cancun Mex, Cozumel Mex,
    Great Stirrup Cay private island, Bahamas.

11) Jan 2-16, 2000 14 Days: Holland Ame. New Amsterdam - Southern Carib. - Tampa -
    San Juan, St. John V.I., St. Thomas, Point Pitre, Guadeloupe
    Bridgetown, Barbados, Castries, St. Lucia, Isla Margarita, Vegas
    Bonaire, Curaçao, Grand Cayman - Tampa

12) Jan 7-14, 2001 7 Days "Costa Atlantica" Eastern Carib. - Port Everglade
    San Juan, St. Thomas, Nassau, Private island (Catalina) Casa de Campo

13) Jan 5-12, 2002 7 Day "Norwegian Sun" - Free Style Cruising". Western Carib.
    Miami, Grand Cayman, Belize, Roatan (Honduras),
    Cozumel, Miami

④ Jan 4 – 11, 2003   7 Days – "Holland River
                              Zuiderdam" – Eastern Carib. Ft. Lauderdale
                     Half Moon Cay, Bessekera, St. Kitts,
                     St. Thomas, Nassau, Ft. Lauderdale
⑤ Jan 3 – 10, 2004   7 Days – Princess "Golden" – Eastern Carib. Ft. Lauderdale
                     St. Thomas, St. Martin, Princess Cays
                     Ft. Lauderdale _

How About A Cop Story

It was the summer of 1954 and I was working the 8am-4pm shift in the Times Square area of mid-town Manhattan New York city. Yes I was a cop at the time since Oct 1, 1952. My beat was west 42nd to west 45th street, Broadway to 9th Ave. I was standing on the corner of 42nd street and 8th Ave with tourists filling the block. All of a sudden a man came running toward me from Broadway yelling, "officer, Officer" "my wife is being raped – please help me!" I ran down the block and there was a big crowd in a circle and in the middle was a young woman being molested. He had to be at least 6 foot 5 inches.

The young woman was dressed for the summer heat and her top was torn off her and she was screaming. The man walking toward her, saw what he liked and started to touch her. I said to myself when I approached the circle that this guy is going to kill me. I certainly couldn't take my gun out with all those people present so I'll have to fight him. I jumped on him so he released the woman and then the fight started. He got me off him and he knocked me down. I got up and then tried to throw him through the store window which had about 2-3 feet of concrete under it to the ground. Now all this time the people never stepped in to help me. I'll discuss that later. He had no weapon and I kept my gun holstered. The fight lasted at least a half hour and we both were beat. I then heard the beautiful sounds from the radio cars responding to the scene.

There were 4 cars and it took all eight officers to finally subdue him. They double hand-cuffed him and took him first to the station-house to book him and later to the hospital for treatment and I was taken to the hospital to be patched up right away. Now where were the nice young people? They apparently left when the fight started. To jump ahead, the big guy got 6 months in jail for felonious assault on a police officer. Now for the issue if anybody should have helped me or not? I could have had some help from some big fella in the crowd but it didn't happen then nor ever. I retired after putting in twenty-one years.

That incident was part of my job not someone else's. However if a crime is being committed out in the street and you see it thru your window, I think a call to the police should take place. When I was fighting that man in the street, somebody called it in or maybe looked for another cop and told him. It still sounds good when you hear the sirens and know help is coming. I wasn't married then but I know Lorraine would have been pretty mad at those people who stood around and did nothing while the guy is pounding her husband.

1.) NOW THE HORSE GETS ME
2.) LOOK OUT CONRAD!!!

Two more cop stories are ready for telling. New York City had world premieres of motion pictures just like Hollywood. It was June 1954 and they were having Marlon Brando's new movie "On the Waterfront" at the Strand Theater in Times Square. There were klieg lights (those round lights that looked like search lights) limousines pulling up to the red carpets in front of the theater, barriers on the sidewalks to keep the people from trying to get at the stars, 2 mounted police officers in the street to control the mobs of people and then my partner and me out front after parking our radio car in the side street. Things were going well until the star of the movie Marlon Brando came last and people broke the barriers to get to him. A few officers on the sidewalk got to him first and got him in the theater. Outside one of the horses got spooked from the crowd and moved around and neighing and he landed with his hind legs on one of my shoes and I couldn't get him off me. I pounded on his rear end yelling "I'm a cop! I'm a cop". Finally I broke free but he had crushed my left shoe and broke my toes. The mounted officer got the horse under control and the crowd dispersed. There was a hospital a couple of blocks away and they took me there to get aid. Marlon Brando left before the movie and came to see me and made a statement to the press "That these premieres are nice but not if a police officer is hurt." It was a nice gesture and statement. Marlon Brando is one of the good guys. My toes eventually healed and I went back to duty.

NOW WHO'S GOING TO GET ME NEXT!

It was in the mid-sixties and one of the mayor's friends was accosted in the Times Square area. The 8th Ave and the 42nd St area now had to be cleaned up said the spokesman from the mayor's office. My beat was again the 8th Ave. and 42nd St. areas (remember the big guy?) only this time I am in the radio car and our orders are to chase any guys who are hanging around on the corners and to keep them moving. We come west on 42nd St and stop on the southeast corner of 42nd St and 8th Ave. my partner is driving so my side is to the sidewalk. There are 3 guys on the corner. I get out to chase them off the corner and said "Come on fellas, off the corner" Two of them started to move and then the third one too. So I was opening the car door with my right hand when I heard a scream from my partner "Look out Conrad!!" the third guy was moving, but towards me. I had my right hand on the door handle and was off balance when he went for me cursing %^&#*&^ cop. I hit him with my left hand and I heard a bone crack and he dropped and seconds later my partner was on my side of the car and hit the guy with his nightstick and then the guy dropped further till he was out cold on the ground. He was a very big man! My partner took him to night court and I went to the hospital to have my broken hand fixed. And for some reason they took me down to Beth-Israel Hospital on the lower eastside to Dr. Luskin. He just invented a surgical tool to join bones; I guess he wanted to test it on me. You put a pin in a drill of some kind. I don't remember him giving me like a shot or something. Anyway he drilled the pinky and the ring finger; ace bandaged it with about one-quarter inch showing. I don't remember how long I was off for the line of duty injury. I was called to his office on the day he was going to take out the pin after seeing him 3 or 4 times before. I sat at his desk and he was holding the hand. He "accidentally" dropped a pencil on the floor and I bent down to pick it up and at that instant he picked up a pair of pliers from somewhere and having my hand in his he pulled out the pin. I started to sweat, lowered my head and nearly passed out. I started to scream at him asking why he did that and he said he finds that's the easiest way to remove the pin. I carried that pin in an envelope till I moved to my present home after my wife passed away. I don't know where I could have misplaced or lost it but I'm disappointed I don't have it. I might have been the first person he tried it upon.

Wrestling Ends in Riot at Madison Square Garden, N.Y.C.

I'M HURT ONCE MORE

On November 19, 1957 at Madison Square Garden, NYC after the tag-team contest pitting Antonino Rocca of Argentina and Eduardo Carpentier of France against Dr Jerry Graham of Hollywood and Dick Affils of Detroit. A riot broke out immediately after the final exhibition on the professional wrestling program. A tag-team fight is one in which only two fighters are allowed in the ring, but either may call on his teammate by touching him. This is a substitution and the wrestler tagged replaces his partner. Usually one of the teams is deemed the villains and in this case it was the losing team of Graham and Affils. The wrestlers do not stop fighting when the exhibition is over especially when the winners are the crowd heroes. The villains then feign a desire for more battle. However it got out of hand. Graham and Rocca continued to fight until they got angry. Rocca was already bloody and rammed Graham's head against one of the brass ring posts.

Fans who favored Rocca turned against Rocca by this action and climbed into the ring and began throwing bottles and folding chairs that were on the floor ringside. Many of the 12, 987 fans who attended took part in the rioting by dropping chairs from the third floor balcony and threw bottles from the third deck balcony barely missing spectators trying to get out of the Fiftieth Street exit of the building.

Thirty-three policemen from the Garden detail of Special Guards had trouble in moving the crowd out of the arena. New York police were called early in the rioting. My partner and I were dispatched to the Garden to restore order. Instead I was hit on the head with a bottle and my partner suffered a strained back when he was forced against the rail while trying to keep the crowd from pushing close to see what was going on, on the main floor. I was on the main floor with a head wound from one of the thrown bottles. We were taken to the hospital and I was treated from the cuts to my head with five stitches and my partner had a severe back injury that later needed surgery.

There were two arrests for disorderly conduct and my partner and myself were the only injuries. It was the worst riot at the Garden.

As with all the line-of-duty injuries or any sickness for that matter, all sicknesses by the police officer must report to the district police surgeon assigned to you. If you cannot then they call the surgeon and usually he tells the officer to report to him when he can. He then receives a report of your injury or sickness along with having your records. When I called him of my injury and he told me to see him when I feel better and I did. The surgeon had my report when he started to examine my head. After a while I felt warm at my forehead and felt it and my hand had blood on it. I asked him what he was doing and he replied "Your injury report says you had five stitches to close your wound and all I can see is two." I said "With all your poking around haven't you heard of dissolvable stitches?" He said "Oh my goodness, I'm sorry officer I will restitch your head. For my mistake I'll give you two more weeks off after you're healed!"

Now I'm about ready to go back to work and I'm getting headaches and nothing is helping. The dept wants me to go back to work and I go out sick again. Now they said I was going to be charged with malingering, so on my own I went to a headache clinic in the Bronx which was supposed to be one of the best on the east coast and told them my problem and any paperwork I had on my head. They gave me all kinds of tests well over a month and their conclusion was I indeed had headaches and indeed they came from the bottle hitting me on the head.

I demanded an apology from the medical bureau of the police dept and guess what. After a few months and plenty of letters from the headache clinic I got one!

Stroke & Dementia

Between October 31 & November 1, 1998 my wife had a stroke of the right vertebral artery dissection (brain stem syndrome) and right medullary infarct associated with Wallenberg left carotid problem. These events occurred while she was in Roper City Hospital, after a successful colon operation. Her ICU and rehabilitation was covered in previous chapters. I now would like to discuss Dementia the horrible disease that destroys your brain. Stroke are one of the causes for dementia or as called in years previous "being senile". In 2005 following the aforementioned strokes my Lorraine was diagnosed with dementia by a doctor in Baltimore Maryland. This doctor was recommended to us by Bear Haven Hospital also in Maryland. She has been seeing this doctor for about a year at this point. She was cold all the time and no doctors we have seen thus far has been able to help her. We searched so far as to contact the Miles Martin Center in Rochester, MN. The doctors at the Miles Martin Center asked us to forward her medical records and we were given an appointment and patient ID#. Despite doing everything asked of us we received a letter canceling our appointment with them stating "There are enough good doctors there in Pennsylvania" Confused and desperately seeking help it is then that we turned to the doctor in Maryland. He decided he wanted to administer a test to see if her sweat glands were working properly. This test was done at his office. There were 2 adjoining rooms. One room had a slab with buckets of coals nearby, the other contained seating and a computer. He proceeded to instruct Lorraine to undress and lie back on the slab. He then covered her in iodine and baking soda and returned to me in the other room. He informed me the test will take approximately one hour to complete and if she moved from the slab the test will be cancelled and he will not re-administer it. He told me I can view the test and instructed me to stand beside him while he ignited the coals. After a few minutes Lorraine began to scream "I'm burning up, what are you doing to me?" The doctor turned to me and requested I calm her down. I responded to my wife "It will be over soon baby just stay still if you move the test will be ruined, you will be okay". She continued to yell but she didn't move. A half hour later the doctor checked on my wife. She looked like a fresh baked casserole coming out of an oven. The baking soda had turned brown on my wife's skin. The doctor said the test was complete and we entered the testing room. He poured a solution on a towel and wiped her face, then handed it to me and asked if I would finish cleaning her. When we were finished and she was dressed we walked into the doctor's office. After a quick view at some papers he said the test seemed good and to return in 5 days for results. We returned 5 days later with lifted spirits only for him to say "Like I thought the test came back good. I don't know what else I can do for you" and he turned and walked out of the room. I was not satisfied with his answer so I leapt to my feet and followed him into the hall. I asked why he just left it like that he replied "Her sweat glands are normal but it is her brain. She has a severe case of dementia" he turned around and continued walking. I stood there lost and confused wondering "What is Dementia and how will it affect Lorraine?"

Since that day I've done as I always have for Lorraine, I loved her, supported her, and took care of her like nobody else could. We would ride around and she loved every minute of it. We would enjoy the scenery as I would sing "big band" songs to her. And to help with her chills we kept the house very warm. In the middle of the night she would be sweating so bad her nightgown would be soaked thru and she would take it off and give it to me to wash for her. As the years progressed she forgot how to put it back on by herself. Then she forgot what a dryer was. The house was so warm I stuck a fan in the spare room and I would go there when I needed to cool down. Every so often Lorraine would get up to come looking for me, walking around calling to me "where are you?". I would gather her up and take her back to the room and lay with her. Just to hold her until she fell back asleep.

Lorraine also loved to walk but because of her condition she couldn't go out by herself. Every day after our car ride I would drop her off at the end of our street and ride behind her as she walked to our house. This continued until she started getting hallucinations. The voices in her head told her to stop eating, stop going to the bathroom, and to stop taking her medication. We still went for our daily rides. Every day the same routine. Leave the house by noon; go to Target where she could use the bathroom, then go and visit our friend Tye-Dye Dave at his shop, Turkey Hill for a sandwich and soda, then on our way home we would stop at the Crossings so she could use the bathroom. For a while everything was fine until "the voices" told her not to go to Turkey Hill anymore so we switched and started going for pizza. As her memory deteriorated I had to show her on holidays the stores were closed. She didn't understand so I would drive her to all the parking lots so she could see for herself. Her stories of "the voices" continued to get worse. I was now making dinner and having to throw it out because they told her not to eat. As time passed I realized that even though she is a strong woman I feared for her health and wellbeing because of her "voices". I brought her under her own power on Oct 7th 2009 to Crater Memorial Hospital to be checked-out. This was another "day of "infamy"

I Had no Knowledge of What Dementia Does

I noted in an earlier chapter the places I took my wife for relief of her disease: Jefferson Hospital in Philadelphia, Geisinger in Danville, Morganville, and Cedar, all in the state of Pennsylvania and to a doctor in Baltimore, Maryland. They were all neurologists. The neurologist in Baltimore is the one who gave her the thermal test which showed her sweat glands were normal. It was also the doctor in Baltimore who diagnosed her with severe Dementia in 2005. Nobody, but nobody ever explained to me what Alzheimer or Dementia were: what the course of the disease was, what to expect and that there was no cure.

Could it be that the array of doctors I took my wife to see knew less than me or was it too much to ask for them to take a little of their time to help me deal with her sickness. Even a pamphlet would of helped some. They all were disgraces to their profession. They didn't give me the courtesy of at least talking to me instead of saying "There isn't anything I can do" and walk away from me.

Even our own family doctor, Dr. Camel said nothing except to put her in a nursing home. He did nothing to help her and in fact ultimately killed her with the Zyprexa, knowing she would die from it because the FDA said she would. It was given to her behind my back with no discussion.

THE COMPLAINT AGAINST
THE DOCTOR

THE COMPLAINT AGAINST THE DOCTOR

The complaint against the doctor includes;

1. The story of what happened and what Dr. Camel did to my wife

2. The reading of my wife's medical records by a hired nurse from a pharmaceutical company

3. My wife's medication including the Zyprexa, a page with the dosage given to my wife

4. The ":Black Box" warnings of 2006 and 2008 against giving the drug to elderly people with dementia and psychosis, which was my wife's condition, because it leads to death

5. The Study of the pharmaceutical company that's makes Zyprexa including the FDA decision to not approve Zyprexa for elderly patients diagnosed with dementia and psychosis because they die from it. Dr Camel gave it to her anyway and she , my wife, died from it.

My wife died from Aspiration Pneumonia, not dementia on December 31, 2009 at Little Forks Hospital two and a half months after Dr. Camel gave her the Zyprexa on the first day of being admitted to Crater Memorial Hospital on October 7, 2009

Rev. 09/2003

COMMONWEALTH OF PENNSYLVANIA
DEPARTMENT OF STATE

(FOR OFFICIAL USE ONLY)

In order for the Department of State to initiate an investigation of possible violations of the licensing, registration, certification or notary commission laws and regulations of the Commonwealth by a licensee, registrant, certificate holder or notary commission holder of the Department, the complainant must complete both sides of this form. Complaints should be typewritten or clearly printed in black or blue ink. Please state the facts briefly and clearly and be sure to submit any documents you have to support your complaint. Sign this form

THIS FORM MUST BE SIGNED AND FILLED OUT COMPLETELY IN ORDER TO BE PROCESSED.

TYPE OF COMPLAINT (PLEASE CHECK ONE): ☐ NOTARY   ☐ ATHLETIC COMMISSION   ☐ CHARITY

☒ PROFESSIONAL/OCCUPATIONAL LICENSE/CERTIFICATE/REGISTRATION   ☐ OTHER

A. COMPLAINANT INFORMATION

LAST NAME	FIRST	MIDDLE INITIAL
	Stuart	

CITY	COUNTY	STATE	ZIP CODE

TEL. (Include Area Code) (HOME)	(WORK)
	RETIRED

B. COMPLAINANT'S ATTORNEY, IF ANY.

LAST NAME	FIRST	MIDDLE INITIAL
STREET ADDRESS (Number and Name)		

CITY	COUNTY	STATE	ZIP CODE

TEL. (Include Area Code)	FIRM NAME

C. NAME AND ADDRESS OF WITNESS, IF ANY.

LAST NAME	FIRST	MIDDLE INITIAL
STREET ADDRESS (Number and Name)		

CITY	COUNTY	STATE	ZIP CODE

TEL. (Include Area Code)	If needed, is this witness willing to support your complaint by appearing at a hearing? ☐ YES ☐ NO

D. NAME AND ADDRESS OF SECOND WITNESS, IF ANY.

LAST NAME	FIRST	MIDDLE INITIAL
STREET ADDRESS (Number and Name)		

CITY	COUNTY	STATE	ZIP CODE

TEL. (Include Area Code)	If needed, is this witness willing to support your complaint by appearing at a hearing? ☐ YES ☐ NO

NOTE: If additional witnesses are available, list names, addresses, and other pertinent data in a manner similar to above on 8 ½ x 11" paper.

E. ARE YOU WILLING TO APPEAR AT A HEARING IN HARRISBURG IF NECESSARY? (YES) NO

DEFENDANT INFORMATION

F. BUSINESS ESTABLISHMENT INVOLVED, IF ANY.

LAST NAME	FIRST	MIDDLE INITIAL
STREET	Name	

CITY		

TEL. (Include Area Code)	PROPRIETOR

G. INDIVIDUAL INVOLVED, IF ANY.

LAST NAME	FIRST	MIDDLE INITIAL
STREET		

	COUNTY	STATE	ZIP CODE

TEL. (Include Area Code)	LICENSE/REGISTRATION/ CERTIFICATE/COMMISSION TYPE AND NUMBER IF KNOWN

1

Rev. 05/2003

H. FOR NOTARY COMPLAINTS ONLY:

Expiration date of notary's commission if known (this date should appear on the notary's stamp, printed beneath the notary seal):	Date of transaction for which this complaint is being filed:

I. DESCRIPTION OF COMPLAINT.

Please describe your complaint in detail below. List services provided by the licensee, registrant, certificate holder or commission holder. Provide dates. List fees paid for notary services, if applicable. Attach copies of related documents and receipts obtained during the course of the matter if possible. If you need more space, please continue on page 4 of this form and/or use additional 8 ½ x 11" sheets of paper if necessary.

Please see the attachments

Rev. 05/2003

J. RESOLUTION.

How would you like this complaint to be resolved?

REVOKE HIS LICENSE

If additional space is needed, please attach 8 ½ x 11" sheets.

K. COMPLAINANT'S VERIFICATION.

I verify that the facts and statements set forth in this complaint are true and correct to the best of my knowledge, information and belief. I understand that statements in this complaint are made subject to the criminal penalties of 18 Pa.C.S. §4904 relating to unsworn falsification to authorities.

_____
(FIRST COMPLAINANT'S SIGNATURE)
DATE: 3-27-10

X _____
(SECOND COMPLAINANT'S SIGNATURE, IF ANY)
DATE:

X _____
(SIGNATURE OF PERSON COMPLETING THIS FORM,
IF OTHER THAN COMPLAINANT)
DATE:

RETURN COMPLETED FORM TO:

L. RECORDS RELEASE (PLEASE COMPLETE IF IT APPLIES TO YOUR COMPLAINT).

TO WHOM IT MAY CONCERN:

THIS WILL AUTHORIZE _____
(name of physician, practitioner, hospital or clinic)
to release to the Department of State and its authorized representatives any pertinent medical records and copies of x-rays relating to

_____
(patient's name)
for the purpose of investigating a complaint.

Signature _____
Date: March 27, 2010

Witness _____
Date: 3/27/10

3

Rev. 05/2003
DESCRIPTION OF COMPLAINT (CONTINUED FROM PAGE 2)

If additional space is needed, please attach 8 ½ x 11" sheets.

Please do not write in this space.

4

COMPLAINT

am making this complaint on behalf of my deceased wife,
who was treated horrendously and neglectfully by
during the period of October 7, 2009 to October 26, 2009.

On October 11, 2009 Dr   gave my wife and overdose of the medication olanzapine, also known as ZYPREXA, 10 milligrams (mg). It was given at 10 PM, Sunday, and she slept from that time until approximately 7 AM, Tuesday morning, about 33 hours. I was at her bedside from 7 AM on Monday, October 12, till she awoke. This antipsychotic medication was given to a 76-year-old elderly lady with memory problems and dementia and psychosis, and a history of a stroke in late 1998. That many hours did a lot of damage to her brain. From the time she woke from this induced state she never spoke, walked, ate, swallowed. I had a PEG for feeding put into her stomach 3 days before being discharged from the hospital. On December 31, 2009, she died for aspiration pneumonia at   . Hospital, the way she awoke on Tuesday October 13, 2009.

My wife had dementia and she was a functioning human being. She developed hallucinations and I felt she should go to the hospital to be checked out. We were admitted from Dr   s office. While waiting in a room at the office for a bed at the hospital,   was in some distress and we needed some assistance and Dr   never came into the room when I called for help. Instead he sent in a nurse (the regular nurse was not there) whose job at this time was to get   out of the office. The bed became available and that nurse got a wheelchair and got   out and to the elevator to my car to be taken to the hospital. The nurse was rough on   securing her safety belt. The nurse took the wheelchair and went back into the building. When we arrived at the hospital,   walked to the admitting desk under her own power.

The first and second days I met with Neurology and Psychiatry under the direction of Dr   . It was agreed she would be put on Exelon Patch (rivastigmine transdermal system) 4.6 mg for the memory. She was frail and could not tolerate high doses of any medication and since she was on the patch and appeared okay and not drowsy I was satisfied my concerns about her were being taken care of. I had told them in no uncertain terms that   entered the hospital under her own power and I wanted her to leave that way. I didn't want her doped up or made a zombie. I had no idea that Dr   had her on olanzapine or any other medication until during her sleep of more than 2 days when I asked the nurse what she was on and she told me olanzapine 10 mg. I did not know she was on any medication except the patch. I asked the nurse who ordered it and she said "Dr   ." My wife should not have been on it at all. She was his patient and I was as well since 1997 and he knew she couldn't tolerate high doses of medication but gave it to her anyway.   never   any trouble. She saw him once a year for her vitals. Her heart was always strong and her blood pressure normal.

October 7, 8, 9, 10 and mid-11th she was eating and going to the bathroom with assistance and talking to herself. Then the overdose two days before she was to be discharged to go home with assistance in place to take care of her. Doctors are supposed to help their patients and keep the families informed of what medications are being given to her. Neither Dr   , nor anyone else at any time ever consulted with me about her medication. In fact, I repeat, I didn't know he was giving her any medications, aside from the Exelon.

On October 11, 2009 at 10 PM everything changed when he gave her that overdose of antipsychotic medicine, Zyprexa. I tried to reach him and he never showed until Tuesday evening between 5-7 PM. However, on the day before, on Monday, when she slept the entire day, I noticed a blue band on her wrist and asked the nurse what that was and she said "DNR" and I said "What? I never ordered that or agreed to it or signed for it. Who did?" I noticed Dr   , Dr   's partner, and asked him who ordered it and he looked through the book and he said "Dr   " I said that was a lie, I would never order that for my wife, take it off. He wrote something and had it removed. Dr   lied about the DNR and from that time on Tuesday told me to reinstate it and I told him to keep her alive.   showed great courage and fought to stay alive.

Dr   had my wife on Zyprexa, which, I have since become aware, is not approved by the FDA for her condition of dementia and psychosis. That very dangerous Zyprexa causes death and of the listed causes is aspiration pneumonia, which   died from on December 31, 2009 in   Hospital. He gave her this deadly medication time and again, despite warnings from the FDA and the simple fact that Zyprexa is not approved for her condition. That's arrogance in its worst form. If I was consulted by him or psychiatry I would never have allowed them to give it to her.

Getting back to Tuesday, his lies and deceit and misconduct were taking place. The horror started. He didn't want to see her anymore. He came to the room and stood at the door until I urged him to come and see   . After all you did that to her! I had first yelled at the nurses for doing nothing. The IV pole was empty and I yelled to them and him when he came "Is everybody waiting for her to die! Do something for her. At least see if she is still alive." I'll never forget those empty eyes of hers staring upward. She hadn't had any food or water since Sunday evening! He just didn't care about her and denied her existence.

She then had a stroke, probably while sleeping, and then Dr   started to work on me to "put her down." Again he said to reverse the DNR. After the stroke her oxygen level dropped and he didn't want me to put her on the ventilator. He said "Would you want to look like that?" and I said "You did it." I asked him why he gave her that overdose and he said "she was agitated and I gave her too much." I told him that she was not agitated because "I was with her the whole day and she was not agitated, she was talking to herself." I then asked him if Neurology or Psychiatry had anything to do with it and he said no, it was his own decision. I then said that "we were going home today, Tuesday, October 13, 2009. Why didn't you let us go in peace?" Again, he said she was agitated. After   was off the ventilator she rallied pretty good and I wanted to have a PEG tube put into her stomach to feed her and he said that was not humane and was against it. I said to Dr _____, the surgeon who was in the room, to "put the PEG in or she will die from starvation." Dr _____ then kept away from me and sent Dr _____ to ICU and to her room. I wanted to get her strong and bring her home but that was impossible. Dr _____ saw to that. So I was forced to put her in a nursing home. Dr _____ took the quality of her life from her. She was functional when she walked into the hospital under her own power and was now a vegetable done by him. It was so important to me that whenever she was going to die that it be at home. Again Dr _____ made that impossible. He laid the foundation for a stroke at _____, oxygen level drop, pneumonia, the PEG and another stroke and the rest at the nursing home.

On October 26, 2009, I made arrangements in the AM for the nursing home and Dr _____ made us wait over 3 hours and finally sent Dr _____ to discharge us. He was afraid to face me and couldn't look at her because he did it.

One morning when _____ was at the nursing home I went with a power of attorney to the Correspondence Department in the Patients' Records Office at _____ to obtain a copy of the DNR document from _____'s records that Dr _____ said I wanted and changed my mind. The young lady in charge checked the computer and said it was not there. I said "it has to be in her file," and she again looked and again said it wasn't there. So where was it? The cover-up was evident. Dr _____ had the blue band put on her wrist and thought she would die and then, when she lived he pulled it out of the file and destroyed it. He had to because I never signed for it. Who else could it have been? Dr _____ then lied when he wrote "the patient's husband changed his mind from DNR to full status." He said that numerous times.

I never wanted DNR for her at all, never asked for it or signed for it so I didn't change my mind because I never had it (the DNR). It was never an option for my wife. This was part of Dr _____'s cover-up to make it appear that I had wanted the DNR for her and then changed my mind. He stayed away and seemed to give the responsibility of my wife's care to Dr _____ It was clear Dr _____ was trying to cover up his big blunder with the medication and his terrible conduct thereafter with his lies. I lost my wife on December 31, 2009 at _____. Hospital in the same condition as when she came out of the 33 hour sleep and I cry for her every day. He made my wife suffer for 2 months before she died.

If he didn't want to deal with _____ he should have told me so and I would have taken her to another doctor. It would have been that simple. Dr _____ overdose of _____ kept her in a bed-ridden state that didn't allow her to get well; neither at _____ or the nursing home in _____ My wife died of aspiration pneumonia at _____ Hospital on December 31, 2009. Dr _____ never gave my wife a chance to come home.

My biggest regret was trusting him because ultimately he betrayed me, betrayed my wife whom I entrusted to him, and ultimately caused her to lose her life and he betrayed his oath as a doctor.

He should lose his license for his conduct which included tampering with patient records and hospital property, for having no ethics, and lying and neglect. He is a disgrace to the medical profession. He took away from me what I most treasured in the world: my dear wife of 37 years. Now take away from him what he probably treasures most: his license.

Respectfully Submitted,

_____

Mar 27, 2010
_____
Date

Review of medical records obtained from.
The records were received as photocopied.

On 07 October 2009 .   ., a 75-year-old female, was admitted to .
          . . . from her physician, Dr .   .'s, office with advanced dementia,
deteriorating over the past several months, presenting with increasing agitation and
auditory hallucinations.

On the Physician's Order Sheet there was a nurse's note "✓DNR status" V.O. Dr .
signed by .   . RN, at 1155. Nursing Progress notes stated "pt is a dnr as per Dr
          ." .   . RN. °°°Nowhere in the copy of the medical record was there a
written order for the DNR by any physician. Nowhere in the copy of the medical record
was there documentation of any discussion with the patient or Mr .   . regarding
implementing DNR status. Nowhere in the copy of the medical record was a copy of an
advance directive for Mrs   . °°° Found in the photocopies was a copy of the first
page of the Power of Attorney, signed by .   . on 25 October 2004.

          . was seen by   ., a PA-C from psychiatry, who ordered
discontinuation of haloperidol and the start of Zyprexa (olanzapine), 2.5 mg orally or an
injection, 5 mg orally at night, and 5 mg intramuscularly as needed.

At 2040 it was documented that .   . was yelling loudly and was agitated.
Zyprexa 5 mg was given orally and 5 mg was administered by intramuscular (IM)
injection.

°°°It should be noted that in Sep2006 the FDA required the manufacturer of Zyprexa ,
          and Company, to add a "Black Box Warning" to the labeling document.°°° The
FDA, in Alert for Healthcare Professionals, states:

> FDA Alert [4/11/2005]: Increased Mortality in Patients with Dementia-
> Psychosis.
>
> FDA has determined that patients with dementia-related psychosis treated
> with atypical (second generation) antipsychotic medications are at an
> increased risk of death compared to placebo. Based on currently available
> data, FDA has requested that the package insert for Zyprexa be revised to
> include a black box warning describing this risk and noting that this drug is
> not approved for this indication.

. . and Company currently has the Black Box Warning on the United States
Package Insert (USPI) describing that:

> . Analyses of seventeen placebo controlled trials that enrolled 5106 elderly
> patients with dementia related behavioral disorders revealed a risk of death
> in the drug-treated patients of between 1.6 to 1.7 times that seen in placebo-
> treated patients. Over the course of a typical 10-week clinical trial, the rate

death in drug-treated patients was about 4.5%, compared to a rate of about 2.6% in the placebo group. Although the causes of death were varied, most deaths appeared to be either cardiovascular (e.g., heart failure, sudden death) or infectious (e.g., pneumonia) in nature. ZYPREXA (olanzapine) is not approved for the treatment of patients with dementia-related psychosis.

On 08 October 2009 it was documented that the DNR bracelet was on. received an IM injection of Zyprexa 5 mg at 1548 and underwent a CT scan at 2052. The CT scan showed mild to moderate atrophy, no acute intracranial hemorrhage, chronic small vessel ischemic changes.

On 09 October 2009, a Psychiatric consultation noted increased agitation. In addition to the Exelon patch, received an injection of Zyprexa at 1124 and oral Zyprexa at 2131. It was documented that the DNR bracelet was on.

A nursing note on 10 October 2009 stated that was unresponsive to all stimuli; the DNR bracelet was on. received oral Zyprexa at 2202.

Nursing notes on 11 October 2009 documented that had not slept the previous night. Dr noted her to be agitated and ordered the nighttime dose of Zyprexa increased to 10 mg. She received oral Zyprexa 5 mg at 1112 and 10 mg at 2242. Routine neurological checks through this date indicated that 's pupils were of normal size, equal, round and reacted briskly to light.

On 12 October 2009 at 1300 Dr noted that was very lethargic and ordered a decrease in the dose of Zyprexa. Additionally he noted her blood pressure as 160/100. Psychiatric consult noted that was sedated the entire day and the nighttime dose of Zyprexa was to be held.

Nursing notes at 0000 stated that the patient was unresponsive; at 0600 her pupils were nonreactive, her limbs were flaccid, she was lethargic, unresponsive to voice, pain, aphasic; at 0830 the nurse was unable to wake the patient and respiratory distress was noted. At 1130 was sleeping, 1450 sleeping, 1600 no change, 1840 no change, 2000 lethargic, pupils nonreactive, 2200 no change, at 2230 her O2 saturation level was low and she was placed on oxygen via nasal cannula.

On 13 October 2009 at 1545 Dr noted that was "…still overly sedated…and perhaps it is a function of not only the one 10 mg dose but accumulative dose since hospitalization." He ordered the discontinuation of Zyprexa.

Pulmonology consult ordered testing and the start of multiple antibiotics for possible pneumonia.

Nursing notes from 0700-1900 reported the patient as lethargic, disoriented to person, place, time; unresponsive to voice, pain, weak extremities. A note at 1700 stated that the patient remained lethargic, unable to tolerate food or fluids. A note at 1800 stated that the patient exhibited severe lethargy, responds to sternal rub only. At 2330 it was documented that the patient remained lethargic.

Dr   noted on 14 October 2009 at 0945   was still very lethargic. After discussion with   , Dr   rescinded the DNR order.   's oral intake was noted as "v poor past few days" and alternative nutrition was ordered. A Pulmonology consult noted that a chest X-ray showed left lung infiltrate and considered the prognosis guarded. Nursing notes state that   finally awoke, briefly, at 1500. By 1630 she was again sleeping and continued to sleep the rest of the day.

Late on 15 October 2009   was transferred to the intensive care unit (ICU), apparently due to unresponsiveness. Her routine neurological check on that date at 2300 showed her right pupil slightly dilated, her left pupil dilated to more than the right, both round, with no note regarding reaction to light. On a Coma Scale she rated 3, the lowest possible rating. She was intubated and placed on a ventilator. A chest X-ray was performed to rule out a pulmonary embolism (PE). No PE was found, the findings were "suspicious for aspiration pneumonia." Additionally, a CT Scan on the 15th found a large right middle cerebral artery infarct with no evidence of hemorrhage. It was unclear exactly when   experienced the stroke. It could have been any time after she was oversedated with the Zyprexa. That is, any time after 2242 on 11 October 2009. The symptoms shown by   after 11 October 2009, the lethargy, limb flaccidity, unresponsiveness, could have been symptoms of a stroke.

From 15 October 2009 until her transfer to a skilled nursing facility (SNF) in   , PA on 26 October 2009   continued to be monitored by Drs   and   , Neurology, Pulmonology, and an Infectious Diseases Specialist, as well as a nutritionist, and occupational therapist, and others. On 23 October 2009 a PEG tube was placed to allow for nutrition, as   was unable to swallow after experiencing the stroke. On that date the Pulmonologist noted that   was in acute respiratory failure and her prognosis was poor. On 24 October 2009 the Neurologist noted that there was no improvement in her status and her prognosis was poor. On 25 October 2009 Mrs   's respiratory status had stabilized and she was being fed via the PEG tube. Dr   and the Nurse Case Manager cleared   for transfer to the SNF. She was taken by ambulance to the   Nursing   CENTER

Per Mr   ,   expired on 31 December 2009 at   Hospital due to aspiration pneumonia.

Respectfully Submitted,

————————————

27 March 2010

* see end of page for Administration Note

☐ see end of page for Not-Given reason

			10/09/09 Day4					10/10/09 Day5					10/11/09 Day6				
	start/stop	ord	11	15	19	23	03	11	15	19	23	03	11	15	19	23	03

SCHEDULED MEDICATIONS

EXELON PATCH 4.6MG

1 APP TOPL ONCE A DAY	10/06 15:00 10/06 16:11	8															
1 TOPICAL TOPL ONCE A DAY	10/06 15:00 10/06 16:11	8		14:46 DCt					15:25 JRs 8								
4.6 TOPICAL TOPL ONCE A DAY	10/06 15:00 10/06 16:11	8													15:20 MER		

M:PATIENT'S OWN MEDICATION - EXELON PATCH ; 4.6MG APPLY ONE PATCH DAILY

OLANZAPINE ZYDIS (ZYPREXA ZYDIS)

| 5 MG/1 TBOL ORAL AT BEDTIME | 10/07 22:00 10/11 16:12 | 4 | | | 21:31 KBz | | | | | 22:08 KBz | | | | | | | |

M:CAUTION: LOOK ALIKE SOUND ALIKE ; MEDICATION

| 10 MG/1 TBOL ORAL AT BEDTIME | 10/11 16:12 | 9 | | | | | | | | | | | | | | | 22:40 KBz |

M:CAUTION: LOOK ALIKE SOUND ALIKE ; MEDICATION

PRN MEDICATIONS

Acetaminophen (TYLENOL)

| 650 MG/2 TAB ORAL 4 TIMES DAILY AS NEEDED | 10/07 19:00 10/26 16:11 | 2 | | | | | | | | | | | 05:41 KBz | | | | |

M:FOR PAIN / HEADACHE; ADULT MAXIMUM ACETAMINOPHEN DOSE PER IM ; HOURS = 4 GRAMS

OLANZAPINE IM ONLY (ZYPREXA IM INJ)

| 5 MG/2.5 SOLR IM EVERY 8 HOURS AS NEEDED | 10/11 16:20 | 5 | | 11:24 PHz 8 | | | | | | | | | | | | | |

M:*** FOR SEVERE AGITATION ***; CAUTION: LOOK ALIKE SOUND ALIKE ; MEDICATION

EXELON PATCH 4.6MG
   10/10 15:25 JRs * one 4.6 mg patch put on
OLANZAPINE ZYDIS (ZYPREXA ZYDIS)
   10/11 11:12 MER * p r n dose
OLANZAPINE IM ONLY (ZYPREXA IM INJ)
   10/09 11:24 PHz * 8:L Vglut

MEDS

* see end of page for Administration Note
13 see end of page for Not-Given reason

	start/stop	ord	10/12/09 Day:7					10/13/09 Day:8					10/14/09 Day:9				
			11	15	19	23	03	11	15	19	23	03	11	15	19	23	03

SCHEDULED MEDICATIONS

CEFAZOLIN 1 GM/50ML IVPB

| 2 G/100 ML PGBK IV
NOW | x1 Dose | 11 | | | | | | | | | | | 01:3
TLT | | | | |
| | M:FOR TEMP 101.3 | | | | | | | | | | | | | | | | |

EXELON PATCH 4.6MG

| 1 APP TOPL
ONCE A DAY | 10/08 15:00
10/28 16:11 | 5 | | | | | | | | | | | | | | | |
| 1 TOPICAL, TOPL
ONCE A DAY | 10/08 15:00
10/28 16:11 | 6 | | 16:10
LK1 | | | | | 16:30
JLH | | | | | | | | |
| 1 TOPICAL, TOPL
ONCE A DAY | 10/08 15:00
10/28 16:11 | 8 | | | | | | | | | | 14:00
SRH | | | | |
| | M:PATIENT'S OWN MEDICATION - EXELON PATCH ; 4.6MG APPLY ONE PATCH DAILY | | | | | | | | | | | | | | | | |

Levofloxacin 500MG/D5W IVPB.

| 500 MG/100 ML PGBK IV
EVERY 24 HOURS | 10/14 11:00
10/22 11:49 | 13 | | | | | | | | | | | 14:00
SRH | | | | |

Metronidazole/Nss IVPB

| 500 MG/100 ML PGBK IV
EVERY 6 HOURS | 10/14 12:00
10/22 22:00 | 14 | | | | | | | | | | | 14:00
SRH | 18:25
SRH | 23:52 05:33
MAr MAr | |
| | M:CAUTION: LOOK ALIKE SOUND ALIKE ; MEDICATION | | | | | | | | | | | | | | | | |

OLANZAPINE (ZYPREXA)

| 5 MG/1 TAB ORAL
AT BEDTIME | 10/12 22:00
10/13 16:04 | 10 | | | | 13 | | | | | | | | | | |
| | M:CAUTION: LOOK ALIKE SOUND ALIKE ; MEDICATION | | | | | | | | | | | | | | | | |

PRN MEDICATIONS

Acetaminophen (TYLENOL, TYLENOL SUPP)

| 650 MG/1 SUPP RECT
4 TIMES DAILY AS NEEDED | 10/14 00:30
10/20 16:11 | 12 | | | | | | | | | | | 00:49
TLT | | | | 23:52
MAr |
| | M:FOR INCREASED TEMP; ADULT MAXIMUM ACETAMINOPHEN DOSE PER 24 ; HOURS = 4 GRAMS | | | | | | | | | | | | | | | | |

EXELON PATCH 4.6MG
  10/13 16:39 JLH = dose 4.6

OLANZAPINE (ZYPREXA)
  10/12 21:42 SVK 13 Clinical decision *pt is very drowsy

CONTINUED
MR: 30-94-56 ID: 70431481 DOB: 12/04/1933 - Medication Administration Report
Page: 1

ROOM 372-D?

- 41 -

* see end of page for Administration Note

☑ see end of page for Not-Given reason

XXXXX XXXXXXXXXXXX	start/stop	ord	11	15	19	23	03

10/12/09 Day:7

Page: 2

SCHEDULED MEDICATIONS

EXELON PATCH 4.6MG

1 APP TOPL ONCE A DAY	10/08 15:03 10/08 16:11	8				
1 TOPICAL TOPL ONCE A DAY	10/08 15:00 10/08 16:11	8			16:10 LKI	

M:PATIENT'S OWN MEDICATION - EXELON PATCH ; 4.6MG APPLY ONE PATCH DAILY

OLANZAPINE (ZYPREXA)

5 MG/1 TAB ORAL AT BEDTIME	10/12 22:09 10/13 15:08	10				☒

M:CAUTION: LOOK ALIKE SOUND ALIKE ; MEDICATION

OLANZAPINE (ZYPREXA)
10/12 21:42 SVK ☒ Clinical decision *pt is very drowsy

LAST PAGE
MR: 30-94-56   ID: 70431461   DOB: 12/04/1933 - Medication Administration Report
ROOM: *372-LJ*
Page: 2
PRINTED BY: MRSK02 --- DATE----- 11/30/2009

- 42 -

* see end of page for Administration Note
☒ see end of page for Not-Given reason

	start/stop	ord	10/06/09 Day:1						10/07/09 Day:2						10/08/09 Day:3					
			11	15	19	23	03		11	15	19	23	03		11	15	19	23	03	

SCHEDULED MEDICATIONS

Cyanocobalamin INJ VIAL (VITAMIN B-12)

| 1000 MCG/1 ML SOLN IM ONE TIME DOSE | x1 Dose | 7 | | | | | | | | | | | | | | | | | | |

EXELON PATCH 4.6MG

| 1 APP TOPL ONCE A DAY | 10/06 15:00 10/26 16:11 | 6 | | | | | | | | | | | | | | | | | | |
| 1 TOPICAL TOPL ONCE A DAY | 10/06 15:00 10/26 16:11 | 6 | | | | | | | | | | | | | | | 15:01 DC4 | | | |

M:PATIENT'S OWN MEDICATION - EXELON PATCH ; 4.6MG APPLY ONE PATCH DAILY

OLANZAPINE (ZYPREXA)

| 2.5 MG/1 TAB ORAL NOW | x1 Dose | 3 | | | | | | | | | | | | | | | | | | |

M:CAUTION: LOOK ALIKE SOUND ALIKE ; MEDICATION

OLANZAPINE ZYDIS (ZYPREXA ZYDIS)

| 5 MG/1 TBDL ORAL AT BEDTIME | 10/07 22:29 10/11 15:12 | 4 | | | | | | | | | | | 22:36 MB4 | | | | | * | d |

M:CAUTION: LOOK ALIKE SOUND ALIKE ; MEDICATION

POTASSIUM CHL 40MEQ/30ML LIQ (POTASSIUM CHL LIQ 40MEQ/30ML)

| 40 MEQ/30 ML LIQD ORAL EVERY 4 HOURS | 10/06 14:00 10/06 22:01 | 6 | | | | | | | | | | | | | | | | x2 | 21:3 MB4 |

M:CAUTION: LOOK ALIKE SOUND ALIKE ; MEDICATION

PRN MEDICATIONS

Haloperidol INJ VIAL (Haloperidol LACTATE)

| 1 MG/0.2 ML SOLN IM EVERY 4 HOURS AS NEEDED | 10/07 12:00 10/07 14:55 | 1 | | | | | | | | 13:02 AIT | | | | | | | | | |

M:PRN AGITATION

OLANZAPINE IM ONLY (ZYPREXA IM INJ)

| 5 MG/0.5 SOLN IM EVERY 8 HOURS AS NEEDED | 10/07 15:00 10/13 18:59 | 5 | | | | | | | | | | 22:47 MB4 | | | | 15:48 DC4 | 20:52 MB4 | | |

M:*** FOR SEVERE AGITATION ***; CAUTION: LOOK ALIKE SOUND ALIKE ; MEDICATION

Cyanocobalamin INJ VIAL (VITAMIN B-12)
   10/08 15:01 DC4 * S:L Deltoid
OLANZAPINE ZYDIS (ZYPREXA ZYDIS)
   10/07 22:36 MB4 * pt anxious, agitated yelling out loud, med given now
   10/08 22:29 MB4 ☒ See note * pt had im dose at 2050 to keep calm for ct scan brain; pt calm at present. med held
POTASSIUM CHL 40MEQ/30ML LIQ (POTASSIUM CHL LIQ 40MEQ/30ML)
   10/06 15:01 DC4 *
   10/06 18:40 DC4 *
Haloperidol INJ VIAL (Haloperidol LACTATE)
   10/07 13:02 AIT * S:L Glut
OLANZAPINE IM ONLY (ZYPREXA IM INJ)
   10/07 22:47 MB4 * S:L Thigh
   10/08 15:48 DC4 * S:R Deltoid
   10/08 20:52 MB4 * S:R Thigh

ACTIVE ALLERGIES: CODEINE

CONTINUED
MR: 30-94-56   ID: 70431481   DOB: 12/04/1933 – Medication Administration Report

- 43 -

* see end of page for Administration Note
☒ see end of page for Not-Given reason

	start/stop	ord	11	15	19	23	03

10/09/09 Day:4

SCHEDULED MEDICATIONS

EXELON PATCH 4.6MG

1 APP TOPL ONCE A DAY	10/28 18:00 10/28 18:11	8					
1 TOPICAL TOPL ONCE A DAY	10/08 15:00 10/28 18:11	8		14:48 DC4			

M:PATIENT'S OWN MEDICATION - EXELON
PATCH ; 4.6MG APPLY ONE PATCH DAILY

OLANZAPINE ZYDIS (ZYPREXA ZYDIS)

5 MG/1 TBDL ORAL AT BEDTIME	10/07 22:00 10/11 12:15	4					21:31 KB2

M:CAUTION: LOOK ALIKE SOUND ALIKE ;
MEDICATION

PRN MEDICATIONS

OLANZAPINE IM ONLY (ZYPREXA IN INJ)

5 MG/0.5 SOLR IM EVERY 8 HOURS AS NEEDED	10/07 18:00 10/13 16:30	5		11:24 P4 8/ IS			

M:*** FOR SEVERE AGITATION ***; CAUTION:
LOOK ALIKE SOUND ALIKE ; MEDICATION

OLANZAPINE IM ONLY (ZYPREXA IN INJ)
10/09 11:24 PH2 * B.L Vglut

LORRAINE COHEN
ZYPREXA DOSING

ADMITTED.   OCT. 7, 2009

WED.
DAY 1   07 OCT '09   2.5 MG. ORAL 13:34
                         5 MG. ORAL 20:38 } 12.5 MG.
                         5 MG. INJ. 22:47

THURS
DAY 2   08 OCT '09   5 MG. INJ. 15.48
                         5 MG. INJ. 20:52 } 10 MG.

FRI.
DAY 3   09 OCT '09   5 MG. INJ. 11:24
                         5 MG. ORAL 20:31 } 10 MG.

SAT
DAY 4   10 OCT '09   5 MG. ORAL 22:02 } 5 MG.

SUN
DAY 5   11 OCT. 09   5 MG. ORAL 11:12
         LAST DOSE 10 MG. ORAL 22.42 } 15 MG.
         OVERDOSE
                                        (52.5 MG.)
                                           TOTAL

ZYPREXA = IS NOT APPROVED BY THE

FDA FOR ELDERLY PEOPLE WITH DEMENTIA AND

PSYCHOSIS, THEY DIE FROM IT. THE MOST

PROMINENT DEATHS ARE CARDIOVASCULAR AND

INFECTIOUS. MY WIFE HAD DEMENTIA AND

PSYCHOSIS, YET, DR. _____ AND

PAC _____ , PSYCHIATRY, ..

GAVE HER THE DOSES LISTED ON PAGE 1

(ZYPREXA DOSING) WHICH ULTIMATELY CAUSED

HER DEATH FROM ASPIRATION PNEUMONIA

ON DEC. 31, 2009.

FOOTNOTE - MY WIFES DEATH WAS

PRECEEDED BY A CVA (STROKE) OCCURING

10-15-09 THROUGH 10-15-09.

FDA U.S. Food and Drug Administration

Home > Safety > MedWatch The FDA Safety Information and Adverse Event Reporting Program > Safety Information

Safety

Zyprexa (olanzapine tablets) August 2008

Detailed View: Safety Labeling Changes Approved By FDA Center for Drug Evaluation and Research (CDER) — August 2008

The detailed view includes drug products with safety labeling changes to the BOXED WARNING, CONTRAINDICATIONS, WARNINGS, PRECAUTIONS, ADVERSE REACTIONS, or PATIENT PACKAGE INSERT/MEDICATION GUIDE sections. Deletions or editorial revisions made to these sections are not included in this summary. Read about the new physician labeling format [1].

Summary View [2]

Sections Modified

BOXED WARNING

WARNINGS

old

- Increased Mortality in Elderly Patients with Dementia-Related Psychosis
  - Elderly patients with dementia-related psychosis treated with antipsychotic drugs are at an increased risk of death. Zyprexa is not approved for the treatment of patients with dementia-related psychosis (see BOXED WARNING).

Summary of Changes to Contraindications and Warnings

BOXED WARNING

WARNING: Increased Mortality in Elderly Patients with Dementia-Related Psychosis

Elderly patients with dementia-related psychosis treated with antipsychotic drugs are at an increased risk of death. Analyses of seventeen placebo-controlled trials (modal duration of 10 weeks), largely in patients taking atypical antipsychotic drugs, revealed a risk of death in drug-treated patients of between 1.6 to 1.7 times the risk of death in placebo-treated patients. Over the course of a typical 10-week controlled trial, the rate of death in drug-treated patients was about 4.5%, compared to a rate of about 2.6% in the placebo group. Although the causes of death were varied, most of the deaths appeared to be either cardiovascular (e.g., heart failure, sudden death) or infectious (e.g., pneumonia) in nature. Observational studies suggest that, similar to atypical antipsychotic drugs, treatment with conventional antipsychotic drugs may increase mortality. The extent to which the findings of increased mortality in observational studies may be attributed to the antipsychotic drug as opposed to some characteristic(s) of the patients is not clear. Zyprexa (olanzapine) is not approved for the treatment of patients with dementia-related psychosis (see WARNINGS).

Label approved 08/14/2008 is not available on this site

- 47 -

FDA U.S. Food and Drug Administration

Home > Drugs > Drug Safety and Availability > Postmarket Drug Safety Information for Patients and Providers

Drugs

Alert for Healthcare Professionals: Olanzapine (marketed as Zyprexa)

9/2006: The issue described in this alert has been addressed in product labeling.

FDA Alert [4/11/2005]: Increased Mortality in Patients with Dementia-Related Psychosis

FDA has determined that patients with dementia-related psychosis treated with atypical (second generation) antipsychotic medications are at an increased risk of death compared to placebo. Based on currently available data, FDA has requested that the package insert for Zyprexa be revised to include a black box warning describing this risk and noting that this drug is not approved for this indication.

This information reflects FDA's current analysis of all available data concerning this drug. FDA intends to update this sheet when additional information or analyses become available.

To report any unexpected adverse or serious events associated with the use of Zyprexa, please contact the FDA MedWatch program either online, by regular mail or by fax, using the contact information at the bottom of this sheet.

Data Summary

- Analyses of seventeen placebo controlled trials that enrolled 5106 elderly patients with dementia related behavioral disorders revealed a risk of death in the drug-treated patients of between 1.6 to 1.7 times that seen in placebo-treated patients. Clinical trials were performed with Zyprexa (olanzapine), Abilify (aripiprazole), Risperdal (risperidone), and Seroquel (quetiapine). Over the course of these trials averaging about 10 weeks in duration, the rate of death in drug-treated patients was about 4.5%, compared to a rate of about 2.6% in the placebo group. Although the causes of death were varied, most of the deaths appeared to be either cardiovascular (e.g., heart failure, sudden death) or infectious (e.g., pneumonia) in nature.

Report serious adverse events to FDA's MedWatch either online, by regular mail or by fax, using the contact information at the bottom of this page.

Questions? Call Drug Information, 1-888-INFO-FDA (automated) or 301-796-3400
DrugInfo@fda.hhs.gov

Contact Us

- **Report a Serious Problem**
- 1-800-332-1088
- 1-800-FDA-0178 Fax
  MedWatch Online [1]
  Regular Mail: Use postage-paid FDA Form 3500 [2]
  Mail to: MedWatch 5600 Fishers Lane
  Rockville, MD 20852-9787

Links on this page:

1. http://www.fda.govhttps://www.accessdata.fda.gov/scripts/medwatch/medwatch-online.htm
2. http://www.fda.gov/downloads/Safety/MedWatch/DownloadForms/UCM082725.pdf

These highlights do not include all the information needed to use ZYPREXA safely and effectively. See full prescribing information for ZYPREXA.

ZYPREXA (olanzapine) Tablet for Oral use
ZYPREXA ZYDIS (olanzapine) Tablet, Orally Disintegrating for Oral use
ZYPREXA IntraMuscular (olanzapine) Injection, Powder, For Solution for Intramuscular use

Initial U.S. Approval: 1996

WARNING: INCREASED MORTALITY IN ELDERLY PATIENTS WITH DEMENTIA-RELATED PSYCHOSIS

See full prescribing information for complete boxed warning.
- Elderly patients with dementia-related psychosis treated with antipsychotic drugs are at an increased risk of death. ZYPREXA is not approved for the treatment of patients with dementia-related psychosis. (5.1, 5.14, 17.2)
- When using ZYPREXA and fluoxetine in combination, also refer to the Boxed Warning section of the package insert for Symbyax.

--------------- RECENT MAJOR CHANGES ---------------

Indications and Usage:

Schizophrenia (1.1)	12/2009
Bipolar I Disorder (Manic or Mixed Episodes) (1.2)	12/2009
Special Considerations in Treating Pediatric Schizophrenia and Bipolar I Disorder (1.3)	12/2009
ZYPREXA IntraMuscular: Agitation Associated with Schizophrenia and Bipolar I Mania (1.4)	12/2009

Indications and Usage, ZYPREXA and Fluoxetine in Combination:

Depressive Episodes Associated with Bipolar I Disorder (1.5)	03/2009
Treatment Resistant Depression (1.6)	03/2009

Dosage and Administration:

Schizophrenia (2.1)	12/2009
Bipolar I Disorder (Manic or Mixed Episodes) (2.2)	12/2009

Dosage and Administration, ZYPREXA and Fluoxetine in Combination:

Depressive Episodes Associated with Bipolar I Disorder (2.5)	03/2009
Treatment Resistant Depression (2.6)	03/2009

Warnings and Precautions:

Hyperglycemia (5.4)	03/2009
Hyperlipidemia (5.5)	03/2009
Weight Gain (5.6)	03/2009
Leukopenia, Neutropenia, and Agranulocytosis (5.9)	08/2009
Use in Patients with Concomitant Illness (5.14)	03/2009
Hyperprolactinemia (5.15)	01/2010
Use in Combination with Fluoxetine, Lithium, or Valproate (5.16)	03/2009
Laboratory Tests (5.17)	03/2009

--------------- INDICATIONS AND USAGE ---------------

ZYPREXA (olanzapine) is an atypical antipsychotic indicated:

As oral formulation for the:
- Treatment of schizophrenia. (1.1)
  - Adults: Efficacy was established in three clinical trials in patients with schizophrenia; two 6-week trials and one maintenance trial. (14.1)
  - Adolescents (ages 13-17): Efficacy was established in one 6-week trial in patients with schizophrenia (14.1). The increased potential (in adolescents compared with adults) for weight gain and hyperlipidemia may lead clinicians to consider prescribing other drugs first in adolescents. (1.1)

- Acute treatment of manic or mixed episodes associated with bipolar I disorder and maintenance treatment of bipolar I disorder. (1.2)
  - Adults: Efficacy was established in three clinical trials in patients with manic or mixed episodes of bipolar I disorder: two 3- to 4-week trials and one maintenance trial. (14.2)
  - Adolescents (ages 13-17): Efficacy was established in one 3-week trial in patients with manic or mixed episodes associated with bipolar I disorder (14.2). The increased potential (in adolescents compared with adults) for weight gain and hyperlipidemia may lead clinicians to consider prescribing other drugs first in adolescents. (1.2)

Medication therapy for pediatric patients with schizophrenia or bipolar I disorder should be undertaken only after a thorough diagnostic evaluation and with careful consideration of the potential risks. (1.3)
- Adjunct to valproate or lithium in the treatment of manic or mixed episodes associated with bipolar I disorder. (1.2)
  - Efficacy was established in two 6-week clinical trials in adults (14.2). Maintenance efficacy has not been systematically evaluated.

As ZYPREXA IntraMuscular for the:
- Treatment of acute agitation associated with schizophrenia and bipolar I mania. (1.4)
  - Efficacy was established in three 1-day trials in adults. (14.3)

As ZYPREXA and Fluoxetine in Combination for the:
- Treatment of depressive episodes associated with bipolar I disorder. (1.5)
  - Efficacy was established with Symbyax (olanzapine and fluoxetine in combination) in adults; refer to the product label for Symbyax.
- Treatment of treatment resistant depression (major depressive disorder in patients who do not respond to 2 separate trials of different antidepressants of adequate dose and duration in the current episode). (1.6)
  - Efficacy was established with Symbyax (olanzapine and fluoxetine in combination) in adults; refer to the product label for Symbyax.

--------------- DOSAGE AND ADMINISTRATION ---------------

Schizophrenia in adults (2.1)	Oral: Start at 5-10 mg once daily; Target: 10 mg/day within several days
Schizophrenia in adolescents (2.1)	Oral: Start at 2.5-5 mg once daily; Target: 10 mg/day
Bipolar I Disorder (manic or mixed episodes) in adults (2.2)	Oral: Start at 10 or 15 mg once daily
Bipolar I Disorder (manic or mixed episodes) in adolescents (2.2)	Oral: Start at 2.5-5 mg once daily; Target: 10 mg/day
Bipolar I Disorder (manic or mixed episodes) with lithium or valproate in adults (2.2)	Oral: Start at 10 mg once daily
Agitation associated with Schizophrenia and Bipolar I Mania in adults (2.4)	IM: 10 mg (5 mg or 7.5 mg when clinically warranted) Assess for orthostatic hypotension prior to subsequent dosing (max. 3 doses 2-4 hrs apart)
Depressive Episodes associated with Bipolar I Disorder in adults (2.5)	Oral in combination with fluoxetine: Start at 5 mg of oral olanzapine and 20 mg of fluoxetine once daily
Treatment Resistant Depression in adults (2.6)	Oral in combination with fluoxetine: Start at 5 mg of oral olanzapine and 20 mg of fluoxetine once daily

- Lower starting dose recommended in debilitated or pharmacodynamically sensitive patients or patients with predisposition to hypotensive reactions, or with potential for slowed metabolism. (2.1)
- Olanzapine may be given without regard to meals. (2.1)

ZYPREXA and Fluoxetine in Combination:
- Dosage adjustments, if indicated, should be made with the individual components according to efficacy and tolerability. (2.5, 2.6)
- Olanzapine monotherapy is not indicated for the treatment of depressive episodes associated with bipolar I disorder or treatment resistant depression. (2.5, 2.6)
- Safety of co-administration of doses above 18 mg olanzapine with 75 mg fluoxetine has not been evaluated. (2.5, 2.6)

--------------- DOSAGE FORMS AND STRENGTHS ---------------
- Tablets (not scored): 2.5, 5, 7.5, 10, 15, 20 mg (3)
- Orally Disintegrating Tablets (not scored): 5, 10, 15, 20 mg (3)

2

- Intramuscular Injection: 10 mg vial (3)

-------CONTRAINDICATIONS-------
- None with ZYPREXA monotherapy.
- When using ZYPREXA and fluoxetine in combination, also refer to the Contraindications section of the package insert for Symbyax®. (4)
- When using ZYPREXA in combination with lithium or valproate, refer to the Contraindications section of the package inserts for those products. (4)

-------WARNINGS AND PRECAUTIONS-------
- *Elderly Patients with Dementia-Related Psychosis:* Increased risk of death and increased incidence of cerebrovascular adverse events (e.g., stroke, transient ischemic attack). (5.1)
- *Suicide:* The possibility of a suicide attempt is inherent in schizophrenia and in bipolar I disorder, and close supervision of high-risk patients should accompany drug therapy; when using in combination with fluoxetine, also refer to the Boxed Warning and Warnings and Precautions section of the package insert for Symbyax. (5.2)
- *Neuroleptic Malignant Syndrome:* Manage with immediate discontinuation and close monitoring. (5.3)
- *Hyperglycemia:* In some cases extreme and associated with ketoacidosis or hyperosmolar coma or death, has been reported in patients taking olanzapine. Patients taking olanzapine should be monitored for symptoms of hyperglycemia and undergo fasting blood glucose testing at the beginning of, and periodically during, treatment. (5.4)
- *Hyperlipidemia:* Undesirable alterations in lipids have been observed. Appropriate clinical monitoring is recommended, including fasting blood lipid testing at the beginning of, and periodically during, treatment. (5.5)
- *Weight Gain:* Potential consequences of weight gain should be considered. Patients should receive regular monitoring of weight. (5.6)
- *Tardive Dyskinesia:* Discontinue if clinically appropriate. (5.7)
- *Orthostatic Hypotension:* Orthostatic hypotension associated with dizziness, tachycardia, bradycardia and, in some patients, syncope, may occur especially during initial dose titration. Use caution in patients with cardiovascular disease, cerebrovascular disease, and those conditions that could affect hemodynamic responses. (5.8)
- *Leukopenia, Neutropenia, and Agranulocytosis:* Has been reported with antipsychotics, including ZYPREXA. Patients with a history of a clinically significant low white blood cell count (WBC) or drug induced leukopenia/neutropenia should have their complete blood count (CBC) monitored frequently during the first few months of therapy and discontinuation of ZYPREXA should be considered at the first sign of a clinically significant decline in WBC in the absence of other causative factors. (5.9)
- *Seizures:* Use cautiously in patients with a history of seizures or with conditions that potentially lower the seizure threshold. (5.11)
- *Potential for Cognitive and Motor Impairment:* Has potential to impair judgment, thinking, and motor skills. Use caution when operating machinery. (5.12)
- *Hyperprolactinemia:* May elevate prolactin levels. (5.13)
- *Use in Combination with Fluoxetine, Lithium or Valproate:* Also refer to the package inserts for Symbyax, lithium, or valproate. (5.16)
- *Laboratory Tests:* Monitor fasting blood glucose and lipid profiles at the beginning of, and periodically during, treatment. (5.17)

-------ADVERSE REACTIONS-------

Most common adverse reactions (≥5% and at least twice that for placebo) associated with:

Oral Olanzapine Monotherapy:
- Schizophrenia (Adults) – postural hypotension, constipation, weight gain, dizziness, personality disorder, akathisia (6.1)
- Schizophrenia (Adolescents) – sedation, weight increased, headache, increased appetite, dizziness, abdominal pain, pain in extremity, fatigue, dry mouth (6.1)
- Manic or Mixed Episodes, Bipolar I Disorder (Adults) – asthenia, dry mouth, constipation, increased appetite, somnolence, dizziness, tremor (6.1)
- Manic or Mixed Episodes, Bipolar I Disorder (Adolescents) – sedation, weight increased, increased appetite, headache, fatigue, dizziness, dry mouth, abdominal pain, pain in extremity (6.1)

Combination of ZYPREXA and Lithium or Valproate:
- Manic or Mixed Episodes, Bipolar I Disorder (Adults) – dry mouth, weight gain, increased appetite, dizziness, back pain, constipation, speech disorder, increased salivation, amnesia, paresthesia (6.1)

ZYPREXA and Fluoxetine in Combination: Also refer to the Adverse Reactions section of the package insert for Symbyax. (6)

ZYPREXA IntraMuscular for Injection:
- Agitation with Schizophrenia and Bipolar I Mania (Adults) – somnolence (6.1)

To report SUSPECTED ADVERSE REACTIONS, contact Eli Lilly and Company at 1-800-LillyRx (1-800-545-5979) or FDA at 1-800-FDA-1088 or www.fda.gov/medwatch

-------DRUG INTERACTIONS-------
- *Diazepam:* May potentiate orthostatic hypotension. (7.1, 7.2)
- *Alcohol:* May potentiate orthostatic hypotension. (7.1)
- *Carbamazepine:* Increased clearance of olanzapine. (7.1)
- *Fluvoxamine:* May increase olanzapine levels. (7.1)
- *ZYPREXA and Fluoxetine in Combination:* Also refer to the Drug Interactions section of the package insert for Symbyax. (7.1)
- *CNS Acting Drugs:* Caution should be used when taken in combination with other centrally acting drugs and alcohol. (7.2)
- *Antihypertensive Agents:* Enhanced antihypertensive effect. (7.2)
- *Levodopa and Dopamine Agonists:* May antagonize levodopa/dopamine agonists. (7.2)
- *Lorazepam (IM):* Increased somnolence with IM olanzapine. (7.2)
- *Other Concomitant Drug Therapy:* When using olanzapine in combination with lithium or valproate, refer to the Drug Interactions section of the package insert for those products. (7.2)

-------USE IN SPECIFIC POPULATIONS-------
- *Pregnancy:* ZYPREXA should be used during pregnancy only if the potential benefit justifies the potential risk to the fetus. (8.1)
- *Nursing Mothers:* Breast-feeding is not recommended. (8.3)
- *Pediatric Use:* Safety and effectiveness of ZYPREXA in children <13 years of age have not been established. (8.4)

See 17 for PATIENT COUNSELING INFORMATION and FDA-approved Medication Guide

Revised: 01/2010

FULL PRESCRIBING INFORMATION: CONTENTS*

WARNING: INCREASED MORTALITY IN ELDERLY PATIENTS WITH DEMENTIA-RELATED PSYCHOSIS

[handwritten annotations: "NOT APPROVED FOR ZYPREXA" and "ELDERLY PEOPLE W/PSYCHOSIS THEY DIE!!"]

FULL PRESCRIBING INFORMATION

> **WARNING: INCREASED MORTALITY IN ELDERLY PATIENTS WITH DEMENTIA-RELATED PSYCHOSIS**
>
> Elderly patients with dementia-related psychosis treated with antipsychotic drugs are at an increased risk of death. Analyses of seventeen placebo-controlled trials (modal duration of 10 weeks), largely in patients taking atypical antipsychotic drugs, revealed a risk of death in drug-treated patients of between 1.6 to 1.7 times the risk of death in placebo-treated patients. Over the course of a typical 10-week controlled trial, the rate of death in drug-treated patients was about 4.5%, compared to a rate of about 2.6% in the placebo group. Although the causes of death were varied, most of the deaths appeared to be either cardiovascular (e.g., heart failure, sudden death) or infections (e.g., pneumonia) in nature. Observational studies suggest that, similar to atypical antipsychotic drugs, treatment with conventional antipsychotic drugs may increase mortality. The extent to which the findings of increased mortality in observational studies may be attributed to the antipsychotic drug as opposed to some characteristic(s) of the patients is not clear. ZYPREXA (olanzapine) is not approved for the treatment of patients with dementia-related psychosis [see Warnings and Precautions (5.1, 5.17) and Patient Counseling Information (17.2)].
>
> When using ZYPREXA and fluoxetine in combination, also refer to the Boxed Warning section of the package insert for Symbyax.

1 INDICATIONS AND USAGE

1.1 Schizophrenia

Oral ZYPREXA is indicated for the treatment of schizophrenia. Efficacy was established in three clinical trials in adult patients with schizophrenia: two 6-week trials and one maintenance trial. In adolescent patients with schizophrenia (ages 13-17), efficacy was established in one 6-week trial [see Clinical Studies (14.1)].

When deciding among the alternative treatments available for adolescents, clinicians should consider the increased potential (in adolescents as compared with adults) for weight gain and hyperlipidemia. Clinicians should consider the potential long-term risks when prescribing to adolescents, and in many cases this may lead them to consider prescribing other drugs first in adolescents [see Warnings and Precautions (5.5, 5.6)].

FIRST CONTACT WITH THE LEGAL BUREAU AND SUBSEQUENT CONVERSATIONS WITH ATTORNEY CLARK WAYNE

Complaint against Dr. Camel

File# of case:

December 21, 2010 – Contacted receptionist at the Legal Bureau of the Department of State. The following information was given to me after giving her the complaint file # of the case against Dr. Camel.

The investigation of the complaint has been completed.

September 9, 2010 – Attorney Clark Wayne legal office of the Department of State (PA) was assigned to the case for determination of how to process the complaint if prosecution is warranted. Time frame could be 9-10 months.

Some penalties could be: Loss of License, suspension, warning letter, maybe a fine.

If required you will have to come to Mainburg for a hearing since you checked "yes" on the complaint that you would come to Mainburg to testify against the doctor, if needed you will be notified by letter of the time, date, and room number.

January 4, 2011 -
I called Mr. Clark Wayne, Prosecutor, he told me the following. "The case will be sent to the in-house physician (of 2) who will tell if the case has a valid medical complaint. If it is a viable complaint, it will go to the outside expert physician costing $5, 000.00 to review the case and if the case is good and he is willing to testify that it is a good case and tell what Dr. Camel did wrong and not safe to practice medicine, They will charge Dr. Camel and give him 30 days to answer the charges. Then a hearing is set and I will call to testify. Attorney Wayne then said that he is not my lawyer but will be the prosecutor for the state against Dr. Camel.

I am to call Attorney Wayne on February 1, 2011 and we will see where the case is.

The case went to the lawyers before the prosecutors, Attorney Wayne said the lawyer who read my case made a notation reading "If all this is true, Dr. Camel is in a lot of trouble!"

February 1, 2011 -
Called Attorney Wayne

Still in house – Call in 2 weeks

February 15, 2011 -
Called Attorney Wayne

Monster case preventing my case from going from stack to in-house physicians (3) of them

Call in 2 weeks. Keep calling.

March 1, 2011 -   Called Attorney Wayne

Case still in-house (some doctor has it!)

Call in 2 weeks

March 15, 2011 -   Called Attorney Wayne

Case still in-house

Call in 2 weeks

"If it was in my power, it would be done already."

March 29, 2011 -   Called Attorney Wayne

He said he thought of me last night, and knew I was going to call today.

Case is still in-house

Call in 2 weeks

April 12, 2011 -   Called Attorney Wayne

It is still with the in-house experts. I explained the subpoena business to get Lorraine's photo ID. He said he doesn't prove case by photos of the patient, but through their records and the doctor's negligence.

Right now the experts are still looking at the records in-house.

He said he likes my attitude. I told him I'd do anything he wants me to do to get the doctor who killed my wife.

Call in 2 weeks

April 26, 2011 -   Called Attorney Wayne

It is still with the in-house experts. I thanked him for not using the picture. He said there is no jury, just a judge. It is better for the case if there is evidence from the records, not a picture.

I thanked him again and he said he'd call me right away If there was some news. I said I'm going all the way with him and he said Okay buddy

Call in 2 weeks

May 10, 2011 -   Called Attorney Wayne

It is still with in-house experts. I asked Attorney Wayne, since October is drawing near, and time is running out for malpractice suit, if it was him, would he try for malpractice. He replied that he agreed with my judge friend, that no one will take the case because there is no money to be made or if they did, they will ask for $50,000.00 or more to start the case then keep taking from you. He wished he could fulfill my expectations but it's not up to him now.

Call in 2 weeks

May 24, 2011 –   Called Attorney Wayne

                      It is still with in-house experts.

                      There was a big back log; hopefully he can get us in soon.

                      I have a feeling it's soon, how long have we been talking? Since February 1, 2011!

                      Call in 2 weeks

June 7, 2011 -   Called Attorney Wayne

                      Still nothing – but maybe he'll try another doctor.

                      After much discussion – I said Dr. Camel should do time. He mentioned a classmate of his who is a great guy up this way, Jeremy Neil, who is not tainted and who would file a "Private Criminal Complaint" against Dr. Camel. I said I don't know if I have the strength right now, but I'll think about it, and I'll go all the way with you. I pray for you every night.

                      Call in 2 weeks

June 21, 2011 -   Called Attorney Wayne

                      "Can I call you this afternoon?" I said yes, what time so I know to be home. He replied "how about 2:00 pm?" I said fine. He said he had my number, but to give it to him again, I did. We said goodbye.

A few minutes later I called him and asked if everything was okay, because he sounded ominous and I got scared. He said everything was fine. We said goodbye. A few minutes later he called and said he couldn't wait and told me the expert in-house doctor said that the case had merit and to move on. Mr. Wayne said he was going to look outside for an expert who would be willing to testify! He told me to call back in 1 month, because this would take some time. I told him how happy I was and he said he was too. I told him I'd help him fight and he said he would do all the fighting. I told him again how happy I was to have him and we spoke a while longer and then he said "hang in there buddy." Call me in a month.

July 19, 2011 -   The case was given to an expert from outside. When outside has it, it moves slowly. Politics here, but it won't affect our case. I told him I'm in good health and have complete faith. You'll do all the fighting. He responded Good, that's what I want to hear Conrad!!!!! Call me in a month.

August 16, 2011 -   Called Attorney Wayne. Left a message

August 17, 2011 -   Called Attorney Wayne

No news, if anything happens in the next month I will call.

Call in one month

September 13, 2011-   Called Attorney Wayne

He wants me to call him on Friday morning. He's seeing some people and will see what direction they'll be going. He'll be in Mainburg the next few days.

September 16, 2011 -   Called Attorney Wayne.

He couldn't call me on Tuesday because he was so upset. Wednesday and Thursday he tried to get his supervisors to get another outside doctor expert to read Lorraine's case again, since the doctor who read her case turned in a 5 page report concluding that "there is no deviation from the standard of care." He said the doctor would not testify against Dr. Camel. Therefore the case is dead. His supervisors refuse to have a second expert read the case and not spend the money again. I asked if I could pay for it and he said no. I also asked for a copy of the report and he again said he couldn't. I asked if I had any other recourse and he said I could ask his boss for a re-review. Mr. Wayne was all broken up with the outcome of the case. He said the doctor wrote that Olanzapine is used by the doctors and certain conditions, I said but the FDA has not approved Zyprexa for elderly people with Dementia with psychosis, but he used it on her and she died, from Aspiration Pneumonia 2 months later just as the FDA warning states. Dr. Camel never consulted with me, everything was behind my back.

Mr. Wayne said I would receive a letter and said it was BS. His boss would sign off on it, but his signature (Mr. Wayne) would be on it, but his sentiments would not be his. They were going to close the file with no reasons given, just like that. I tried a few times afterwards but Mr. Wayne would not speak to me, the letter finally came, dated October 11, 2011. I then sent a letter to the ombudsman of the FDA, The FDA, the Attorney General, and nobody wanted to help me. I then wrote to Commissioner Sally Falstaff of the Professional & Occupational Service Department of State and she showed compassion towards my fight for justice for my wife, who died as a result of the doctors actions. I received a letter from her counsel, directing a re-review of the case dated December 9, 2011. A letter from the prosecutor who will read the re-review dated December 1, 2011.

May 1, 2012 (5 months) and no results yet.

July 18, 2012

I received a letter dated July12, 2012 from Attorney Knottingham closing the case against Dr. Camel due to insufficient evidence.

PA RIGHT TO KNOW LAW
OPEN RECORDS OFFICER
RIGHT TO KNOW OFFICER
WHY I FILED FOR RECORDS

On March 27, 2010 I had made an ethical complaint against Dr. Dave Camel of Crater Memorial Hospital for complete neglect and that he be held responsible for her death from Aspiration Pneumonia on December 31, 2009. The complaint was made to the Professional Compliance Office Bureau of Enforcement and Investigation Mainburg, PA 17105.

The whole complaint and timelines are in the rear of the book.

On February 1, 2011 I started to speak to Attorney Clark Wayne in charge of the case to check the status of the case. June 21, 2011 an in-house doctor told Attorney Wayne the case had merit and to move on. This process took 9 ½ months. Now an expert outside doctor was reading the case an 2 months later said "There is no deviation from standard care would not testify against Dr Camel." They were going to close the file. Three months later, after letters and phone calls the Bureau of Professional and Occupational Affairs, Dept. of State Re: reviewed the case and another 8 ½ months of waiting they closed the file citing insufficient evidence.

Now we get to the Right to Know Law, I never heard of it till early to mid November 2012. The good part of this law is that you do not need a reason for the request for information (but try and get it) it is implied that all records are for the people to see and obtain. There is a great case for me in the chapter: why was my case against Dr. Camel closed? Here in the book. If I needed a reason it would be perfect. It deals with the outside dr. and his conversations with Attorney Clark Wayne and the investigator for the state and what is in his report. So I made an application for the records of both parties. You can apply for anything but unfortunately there are restrictions so the denial will take place.

The request for the files of the investigator in the complaint against Dr. Dave Camel.

Answer: The Dept of State has denied your request for the investigative file including any and all report of outside experts. (They are talking about the expert doctor.) Assuming that such records exist (of course it does) the request is also denied because it seeks information related to non-criminal investigations that is exempt from exposure under 67.708 (13)(17) of the Right to Know law. This includes your requests for complaints. If disclosed said records would reveal the institution, progress or result of an agency investigation the Office of Open Records has repeatedly denied the exposure of various types of inspection reports pursuant to this exemption.

I appealed the decision and it was denied again saying briefly documents, materials or information obtained during as investigation conducted on behalf of the State Board of Medicine therefore the requested records are confidential and not subject to public disclosure.- January 15, 2013.

So there again I'm shut down again by the state. Twice by the medical board and once by the Right NOT to Know law! All I ever wanted was justice for my deceased wife and a fair shot at the doctor who caused her death. That's why this book is so important to me. To tell her story and mine.

The outside doctor told Attorney Clark Wayne many facts about Dr. Camel and Marjorie Nelson. PAC psychiatry and Attorney Wayne told me and nobody would listen. Everything told to me can be found in the chapters: Timeline and Why Was My Case Against Dr. Camel Closed? Very damaging evidence against Dr. Camel and the expert outside doctor.

Bureau of Profesional and Occupational Affairs Prosecutorial Division, Department of State

I often repeat myself at times, but it is not an oversight; it is done on purpose because I don't want you to forget why I wrote this book. I don't want the reader to forget what happened to my wife at a hospital and what happened to me at a state agency trying to get the doctor that killed her and whose mission it is to dispense justice and punish the bad guy; not let him go.

It could easily happen to your loved one and this book documents how it happens. Ask lots of questions. You can't always trust your primary doctor who has taken care of you for fifteen years (our family doctor) to make good end-of-life decisions. There are bad cops, bad lawyers, even bad accountants, but whoever thinks of doctors, RN's or any medical staff could be evil? Folks, there are plenty!

This doctor, our doctor, was and is evil. I told the case worker I was taking my wife home on Saturday, October 10, 2009, with assistance. I was going to hire some of the nurses' aides and techs who fed her. The case worker suggested I should wait until the next day when Dr. Camel would be there. I waited until Sunday and told him I was taking her home with assistance. He said to wait until Tuesday and he would discharge her in the afternoon. I figured there was no harm in a couple of days so I agreed. That night he overdosed her with an 10mg of Zyprexa and she already had 5mg during the day. Remember, I knew nothing of what he was doing. It was all behind my back, both he and Marjorie Nelson, PAC Psychiatry. I would come to the hospital every morning at 7:00 am while Lorraine was sleeping. That morning she slept all day and I couldn't wake her. I asked the nurse if she was on anything. She said "Yes" and I asked what and who ordered it. She said Zyprexa 10mg and that it was ordered by Dr. Camel.

I held her hand while she slept for thirty-three hours during which time she had a stroke. I called for Dr. Camel all day, but he never came. He came Tuesday evening between 5:00 pm and 7:00 pm. When she awoke on Tuesday morning, she couldn't walk, talk, eat, swallow or see. That's what he did to my wife. I put her in a nursing facility in Little Forks where she had another stroke and eventually died on December 31, 2009 in Little Forks Hospital from Aspiration Pneumonia.

TIME LINE

The following is what transpired in my pursuit for justice for my wife.

1. March 27, 2010 – Ethical Complaint completed and sent out.

2. April 26, 2010 – Received acknowledgement of complaint and informed that they will investigate.

3. July 19, 2010 – Investigator for the state called and made an appointment to meet me at my home.

4. July 23, 2010 – Investigator came to my home and discussed the case. I signed an authorization form allowing him to obtain my wife's records from Crater Memorial Hospital, Dr. Camel's office, and The Nursing Home of the Angel.

5. August 15, 2010 - I had a chance meeting at the nursing home with the investigator. (I went to the nursing home quite often and still visit frequently.) The investigator stated that he was turning in his investigative report which he said was to be completed in December 2010.

6. December 21, 2010 - I made contact with the Bureau of Professional and Occupational Affairs, Department of State, and was informed that the investigation had been completed and the case was turned over to Attorney Clark Wayne on September 9, 2010.

7. February 1, 2011 -   I started to speak to Attorney Clark Wayne to check the status of the case. An in-house doctor was reading the case and my wife's records.

8. June 21, 2011 -   The in-house doctor told Attorney Clark Wayne that the case had merit and to move on.

9. July1, 2011 -   The expert outside doctor was reading the case now. In order for Dr. Camel to be charged, the expert outside doctor had to say the case was good and agree to testify against Dr. Camel.

10. September 16, 2011 -   The doctor reported there was no deviation from standard of care and refused to testify. They closed the case and I still don't know why.

11. As of December 1. 2011,   after letters and speaking to the Attorney General, FDA, and Ombudsman for the FDA, the Commissioner, Sally Falstaff of the Bureau of Professional and Occupational Affairs, Department of State, directed a re-review of the case.

12. July 18, 2012 -   Received a letter dated July 12, 2012 from Attorney Knottingham closing the case against Dr. Camel due to insufficient evidence.

DECISION NOT TO SUE, TO SUE, AND FINALLY NOT TO SUE

Dr. Camel gave my wife 5mg of Zyprexa at 11:12 am on Sunday October 11, 2009 when I told him on that afternoon I was taking her home with assistance that day. He talked me into waiting till Tuesday afternoon I thought a few more days of rest wouldn't hurt her. It didn't hurt her it killed her because at 10:42 pm that evening he gave her a 10mg Zyprexa overdose. She slept til Tuesday morning and according to neurologist Manual Costas had a stroke with a timeline from October 11 – October 15. When I found out what Dr. Camel and Marjorie Nelson PAC Psychiatry (this is covered to a point in the complaint against Dr. Camel) was giving my wife. I had a decision to make. Raise hell and bring the CEO of the hospital into it or go after the doctor in silence because hospital lawyers would make sure he is protected. I am told by legal minds the decision was correct but after she couldn't talk, walk, eat, swallow nor see. I was going to sue the doctor but after speaking to 5 lawyers, not one wanted the case. After getting her medical records with "Power of Attorney" while my wife was in the Nursing Home of the Angel and still alive. I then knew they were giving her Zyprexa behind my back. There were no discussions about D.N.R. or the medication. The entire picture is made clear in her medical record and this subject is written through the entire book. I tried to get justice for my wife through the medical board and they shut me down twice without looking at my solid evidence that's the surest thing in the case. In September 2012 I started a letter campaign to try to get her story out to no avail. I sent letters to: Nancy Grace, 48 Hours Mystery/Hard Evidence, Jane Velez-Mitchell at CNN, WABC-TV on your side, 20/20, 60 Minutes, The O'Reilly Factor,

Senator P. Casey Jr., Congressman Lou Barletta, Senator Pat Toomey, State Rep. Rosemary Brown, State Rep. Mario Scavello, Senator David Argall, U.S. Sub-Committee on Human Rights Senator John Yudichak. Only representatives of Sen. Toomey, State Rep. Scavello and CNN responded to the which explained my case where my wife was killed by a doctor giving her Zyprexa not approved by the FDA for her condition and my bad treatment by the Bureau of Professional and Occupational Affair, Dept. of State, Mainburg, PA.

The rep. of Mario Scavello called me and we had a discussion on the case and got nowhere.

A staff member of Sen. Pat Toomey called and said Sen. Toomey is federal and does not deal with state agencies. And since my case is a state case he referred me to the Bureau of Professional and Occupational Affairs in Harrisburg. Wasn't that a joke! I told him all that I went through with them over my wife's death. He sympathized with me and mentioned that State Rep. Mario Scavello might be able and I told him I already spoke to his staff member without success. I told him to please tell Sen. Toomey that the gov't. should have hearings about doctors killing patients and I will be happy to testify. You have my address and phone numbers and if it ever happens call me or write me or both. I only want people who bring loved ones to the hospitals for help to be safe and not come home in body bags. Doctors should not have the power they have to do whatever they want to in caring for their patients. Please tell this to Sen. Toomey these are my concerns and whether local, state, or federal gov't. The killing of elderly people must stop and hold doctors accountable. My wife, as I stated in my letter to Sen. Toomey was killed by a doctor giving her medication that he gave against FDA ruling that death occurs if that medication (Zyprexa) is given with her condition (Dementia) and he gave it to her and she died. Thank You.

"CNN" – The third of the 3 who responded to my letter or telephone. I sent out 16 letters certified/return receipt. I received the return receipt of all but apparently none felt my letter of the killing of my wife by a doctor was not news worthy or important enough to reply or help me in my plight for justice for my wife. The letter sent to me from CNN is a nice letter and I think I'll send along a copy of it as an attachment to this chapter of the book. If nothing else at least the courtesy of a letter helps. I guess killing of patients by doctors in hospitals is old news, but it's still happening folks!! Believe me! 3 out of 16 – wow! I didn't think anyone cared when it was happening, now I <u>know</u> nobody cares.

ONE CNN CENTER, Atlanta, GA 30303-2762

VIEWER COMMUNICATIONS MANAGEMENT
vcm@cnn.com

RECD: 11-2-12

October 29, 2012

Hello

Thank you for taking time to share your story idea with CNN. It is important to us that we provide our viewers with news coverage and stories on topics that are of interest to them. One of our best resources for that information is you, our viewing public.

Viewer Communications Management reviews and summarizes story ideas, and distributes them to the appropriate news divisions for consideration. If it is decided the story is something of interest that can be developed for on-air reporting, you may be contacted for more information.

We pride ourselves in helping to maintain the relationship between our viewers and the CNN news teams by sharing your ideas with them. However, because of the volume of story suggestions we receive, we are unable to reply with information on whether or not it will be used.

Thank you again for sending your story idea our way. We look forward to your continued support.

CNN
Viewer Communications Management

A TimeWarner Company

OCTOBER 31, 2011 LETTER TO COMMISSIONER SALLY FALSTAFF

October 31, 2011

Commissioner Sally Falstaff
2601 North 3rd St
Mainburg, PA 17110

Commissioner Sally Falstaff;

I am appealing to you to right a terrible wrong perpetrated against me in the pursuit of justice for my deceased wife. My name is ˜   ˜   , 3 Turtle Cove, Oak, PA 18630. the complaint is against one Dr. David Camel, and the complaint file # is   ˜ ˜ the complaint was filed March 27, 2010 with the Department of State. The Legal Bureau has had the case since September 21, 2010.

My wife had dementia with psychosis and I brought her to Crater Memorial Hospital, Cedar, PA. to be checked out (She came into the hospital under her own power.). On October 7, 2009, from the first day there until he overdosed her on October 11, 2009, he was giving her behind my back, a drug called Zyprexa, which is not approved by the FDA for her condition, putting a DNR on her without my permission, horrible treatment and complete neglect of her to name a few.

I have taken the liberty of providing you with a copy of the complaint to make the situation clearer for you.

The complaint was received by the Compliance Board, Department of State in late March 2010. I received the acknowledgement late April 2010, that the allegations would be investigated. The investigation took place, was completed and sent to the Legal Bureau and the case was assigned to Attorney Clark Wayne September 9, 2010. On June 21, 2011 the in house doctor had called Mr. Wayne, and said the case had merit and to move on. Then an outside expert was given the case on June 28, 2011.

On September 16, 2011, Mr. Wayne told me the doctor turned down the case and refused to testify and Mr. Wayne told me his boss, Mr. Kevin Newman refused to spend anymore money and was going to close the case. Without a re-review of the case. I was stunned because after waiting so long to see the doctor in court because of his lies, willful acts of neglect, his putting a DNR on my wife without asking me (there's more beside the medication Zyprexa was given that caused her death, which also gave her a stroke) they are covered in my original enclosed complaint.

To close the door to my getting justice for my wife is unpardonable.

A few more points: Mr. Wayne told me that prior to him receiving the case the lawyer read it and said " if all this is true, that guy is in a lot of trouble," then after the in-house doctor received the case that " it has merit and move on" and that was after 10 months. The outside man reads it and after only 2 ½ months says "there is no deviation from the standard care" and Dr. Camel told him Marjorie Nelson, PAC, psychiatry initiated the administering of the unapproved Zyprexa to my wife and he didn't know what to do and asked other doctors what to do.

Mr. Wayne asked the outside doctor if he had spoken with Dr. Camel and he said no. Then how did he know about the conversation? And suddenly it was said and confirmed that Dr. Camel closed his Family Practice but retained his practice of Nephrology. What a coincidence! Something is very suspicious and dirty here. This is why I called the office of attorney general for help. After being turned down by the FDA in getting justice for my wife who passed away on December 31, 2009, at Little Forks Hospital of Aspiration Pneumonia from the Zyprexa given to her by Dr. Camel and Marjorie Nelson, PAC Psychiatry, Crater Memorial Hospital.

My enclosed complaint that is still with the Department of State covers the case quite well with no lies. I wonder if anybody has read it after being received at the prosecutor's office.

This was a bad decision by Mr. Newman. I am also enclosing a copy of the letter I wrote to Mr. Newman asking for the letter with the decision of why the case was closed. I never called him relative to re-review because he wouldn't do it for Mr. Wayne, so would he do it for me. The deal was made and done. Please don't let the bad guys win.

Respectfully Yours,

3 Turtle Cove
Oak, PA 18630

Senior Prosecuting Attorney Kevin Newman   November 1, 2011
Department of State
2601 North 3rd St
Mainburg, PA 17105-2649

Dear Sir;

"There is no deviation from the standard of care", is one of the many things told to Mr. Wayne by the Commonwealth Doctor, from the outside. I feel that I must make a reply. "That means it was okay for Dr. Camel and PAC Marjorie Nelson to give my wife 52.5mgs of Zyprexa in the 5 days from October 7, 2009, the day she entered Crater Memorial Hospital under her own power, to be checked out. To October 11, 2009, when the overdose was given and she not only slept for 33 hours, in addition, suffered a stroke from the black box warnings in 2006 & 2008 for elderly people with dementia and psychosis as my wife suffered from, because they die from it and the leading causes of death being cardiovascular (heart) and infectious (Aspiration Pneumonia) which my wife died from 2 months later on December 21, 2009. **AND ALL DONE BEHIND MY BACK!** She also had a stroke in the nursing home. Also that means it was okay for Dr. Camel to put DNR on her without talking to me first, since I was the spouse and my wife could not understand that, with her dementia. This was the first day she was in the hospital and he gave a verbal order to the nurse and the nurse put the DNR on her and signed her name. Dr. Camel then filled her files with lies that I wanted to have a DNR and I changed my mind. I never wanted it; I never asked for it, and most of all, I never signed for it. He also never asked me about it. He expected her to die, but she lived. He took his own signed order out after I had it taken off her wrist by his partner Dr. Little. After asking who ordered it and he looked thru her papers and said "Dr. Camel" I could go on and on about compelling evidence the outside doctor **"FAILED TO SEE!"**

I now request a written explanation of why my case is being closed. It was told to me, September 16, 2011 that the case would be closed and as of yet I have not received a letter, please respond.

Thank you for your consideration in this matter.

3 Turtle Cove
Oak, PA 18630

November 7, 2011

Commissioner Sally Falstaff
2601 North 3rd St.
Mainburg, PA 17110

Dear Commissioner,

I must share with you once again some thoughts concerning my battle to re-open my case against Dr. Camel. I can't let my dear wife become a statistic of those killed and the killer gets away with it as in the OJ Simpson and poor little Kaylee Anthony cases. This time it's the doctor who commits the crime.

I also remember Mr. Wayne asking me months before the October 2011 date of the Statute of Limitations for me to start a mal-practice suit and I said yes I know the date but I have tremendous faith both in the case and in you, and the legal system and I intend to go all the way with you and help you fight , and he said no, I'll do the fighting. I was uplifted by his resolve and confidence and knew in my heart that in just a matter of time Dr. Camel would be found guilty of what ever the charges would be and justice would be served. But lo and behold, the ugly head of corruption buy outs and sell outs rears its ugly head and my faith in the system vanished.

I'll never forget how my wife looked after Dr. Camel's Zyprexa did its job when she opened her eyes after sleeping for 33 hours and had a stroke while sleeping. My beautiful wife was now transformed into lifeless, helpless woman who couldn't walk, talk, eat, swallow, or see. She suffered another stroke at the nursing home where I had to place her. Bouts with pneumonia and finally passing away on December 31, 2009 from Aspiration Pneumonia the way the FDA black box warning said elderly people with dementia and psychosis die if they are given Zyprexa.

From the time I brought her on her own power to the Crater Memorial Hospital til the day she died from Zyprexa was just 2 ½ months. Dr Camel should have that on his conscience but he is amoral.

Ma'am please don't let my dear wife be killed in vain. Please have investigations started of the outside expert doctor, Dr. Camel and anyone else involved in helping Dr. Camel escape prosecution and making a mockery of the justice system. Dr. Camel bought his way out. How could that happen? There was a lot of evidence against him that would easily end in a conviction. I don't know who contacted who but the contact was made and the buy out was made. The expert doctor had papers in his possession. He should have been made to read the papers in the prosecutors office. Those papers should have been protected. The in-house doctor took about 10 months to read them in the office, the expert had the papers about 2 ½ months at home. As I mentioned, there was a mountain of very good evidence in my complaint and the rest of the papers. My wife died at Dr. Camel's hand. Nobody could come to any other conclusion. It's all in the papers presented. Mr Wayne is a good man, and honest, beyond reproach and I believe is a true believer in justice and the American Legal System.

It is my understanding from Mr. Wayne that the expert outside doctor responded that Dr. Camel blamed Marjorie Nelson PAC who initiated the Zyprexa. I have read this nowhere in the doctor's records or conversations.

Attached is a copy of the letter I received on November 5, 2011. And there were no reasons given for the closing of the file.

I appreciate your time and attention to this matter.

Yours truly,

3 Turtle Cove
Oak, PA 18630

COMMONWEALTH OF PENNSYLVANIA
GOVERNOR'S OFFICE OF GENERAL COUNSEL

.n@state.pa.us

Prosecuting Attorney

October 31, 2011

Re: , M.D.

Dear Mr.

Thank you for filing the complaint in the above case. As we discussed, after reviewing the allegations, the decision has been made to close our file. Please note, however, that the file may be reopened if additional information becomes available or if a physician with a surgical specialty is sued four times within a two-year period, or if a physician with a non-surgical specialty is sued two times within a two-year period. Of course, as I indicated on the phone, you may have your file re-reviewed upon request.

It has been my pleasure working with you on this file, getting to know you and learn about your lovely wife. If you have any questions about the decision to close the file (or anything else for that matter), please feel free to contact me at the number below.

Sincerely,

Prosecuting Attorney
Commonwealth of Pennsylvania
Department of State

- 76 -

Commissioner Mary McBride   November 8, 2011
Food and Drug Administration
5630 Fishers Lane
Room 10-61
Rockville, MD 20857

Dear Commissioner,

My name is   ; on October 18th, 2011 I spoke with a very nice lady named Lindsey, from Ombudsman for the FDA. My problem then and still is today, is that I can't understand why the FDA can't police there rulings.

My wife had Dementia and Psychosis. I took her to the local hospital, Crater Memorial Hospital. Under her own power on October 7, 2009, just to check her out because she was not eating or taking her medication. I was afraid for her health since she was losing weight. The first day in the hospital I met with the psychiatry and neurology departments under the direction of Dr. Dave Camel, I told him in no uncertain terms that I did not want her doped up or made a zombie and the only medication was to be Excelon patch for her memory. They said okay, but ignored my wishes. Behind my back they put her on Zyprexa, which the FDA has said is not approved for elderly people with dementia and psychosis, because they die from it. My wife was 75 years old at the time. The black box warning said deaths were varied but the most prominent deaths were cardio-vascular (heart) and infectious (Aspiration Pneumonia). My wife was given 52.5mgs from October 7, 2009 until October 11, 2009. A double dose in the evening. She then slept for 33 hours, had a stroke at the same time. When she opened her eyes, she couldn't see. Couldn't eat, talk, walk or swallow. Dr. Camel made her into a helpless woman. He should have never given her Zyprexa, because the FDA had not approved it for her condition. She also got Pneumonia at CMH and I then had to put her in a nursing home, where she had another stroke, bouts with Pneumonia and passed away, December 31, 2009. She was killed from the Zyprexa just as the warning stated. Killed by the Dr. Camel. She had Dementia with Psychosis, but was a functioning woman.

I made a complaint against Dr. Camel with the state, charging professional misconduct. (No lawyers wanted the case.) I received word that my case would be closed with no reasons given. Bad and dirty doctors betrayed me and no justice for my wife, because of a pay off. He violates your ruling by using Zyprexa, causing her death and pays a dirty doctor off to avoid prosecution.

I turn to you for help to get justice for my wife and to bring Dr. Camel to justice.

Yours truly,

3 Turtle Cove
Oak, PA 18630

COMMONWEALTH OF PENNSYLVANIA
GOVERNOR'S OFFICE OF GENERAL COUNSEL

*/@pa.gov

Executive Deputy Chief Counsel

November 9, 2011

3 Turtle Cove

    RE: Your complaint against   , M.D.

Dear Mr.

    As Executive Deputy Chief Counsel to the Pennsylvania Department of State's Bureau of Professional and Occupational Affairs, I serve as counsel to Commissioner   for all matters within the jurisdiction of the Bureau. She has forwarded your letter to her dated October 31, 2011, to me for review.

    Although I am confident that your complaint against your wife's physician was handled properly, in response to your letter I have directed that your complaint be reviewed again. The review will be conducted by a different prosecuting attorney who will make an independent evaluation of our complaint. That evaluation will then be reviewed by a supervising attorney.

    We will, in due course, advise you of our findings and/or determinations.

        Sincerely,

        Executive Deputy Chief Counsel
        Commonwealth of Pennsylvania
        Department of State

TNG/
CC: Commissioner, BPOA

DEPARTMENT OF STATE / OFFICE OF CHIEF COUNSEL
2601 NORTH 3RD STREET / P.O. BOX 2649 / HARRISBURG, PA 17105-2649
PHONE: 717-783-7200 / FAX: 717-787-0251 / WWW.DOS.STATE.PA.US

COMMONWEALTH OF PENNSYLVANIA
GOVERNOR'S OFFICE OF GENERAL COUNSEL

- Prosecuting Attorney   E-Mail:a   ßstate.pa.us

Date: DEC 0 1 2011

3 Turtle Cove

RE:

M.D.

Dear Mr.

   I am the Supervisor from the Department of State Legal Office and I have commenced the re-review of your complaint. Commissioner   e received the packet of material from your November 28, 2011 and she wanted you to know that it will included in your complaint.

   We appreciate your efforts in filing the complaint. Our office takes such complaints very seriously. I understand that you lost your wife and are grieving that loss. I am truly sorry about that loss.

   Thank you for taking the time to file the complaint. I will be in touch when I complete the review.

Sincerely,

Prosecuting Attorney
Commonwealth of Pennsylvania
Department of State

CC:

DEPARTMENT OF STATE/OFFICE OF CHIEF COUNSEL
2601 NORTH 3RD STREET/P.O. BOX 2649//HARRISBURG, PA 17105-2649
PHONE: 717-783-7200/FAX: 717-787-0251/ WWW.DOS.STATE.PA.US

June 5, 2012 – 8:15am

I called the Legal Bureau and asked to speak to Attorney Knottingham. The receptionist asked for my name and what the call was in reference to. I said my name is ⸱ and Commissioner Sally Falstaff asked Attorney Knottingham to review my Ethical Complaint against Dr. Dave Camel, File ⁿ ⁱ ⁹⁻⁻²⁻⁰ⁿ, ⸱ and I would like to know the status of the case since it is now 6 months that he is reading it.

The receptionist said he was in and she would g to his office and tell him. She then said if you get his voicemail, then tell him in your message everything you just told me. His voicemail came on and I related everything I just said to her and also gave him my home number and my cell number and asked him to please return my call and thanked him.

June 12, 2012 – 8:13am

I called the Legal Bureau and the receptionist asked if she may help me. I asked for Attorney Knottingham. I then said your name is Christina, isn't it? I remember your voice. She said yes and you're ⸱ ⸱⸱ You've always been respectful of me and me to you let me see if he's in his office. He's around here somewhere.

After a few moments his voicemail came on and I said I'm Stuart Cohen, Mr Knottingham and I called last week. You're reading case file ⸱⸱ ⸱ ⸱⸱ ⸱ ⸱. I'd like to get a status report of the case. Please return my call. I then gave him my home number and cell phone numbers again and said thank you.

As of June 20, 2012, I have not yet received any returned calls from Mr. Knottingham.

June 21, 2012

Attorney Alex Knottingham
Dept of State / Office of Chief Counsel
2601 N. 3rd St
P.O.Box 2649
Mainburg, PA 17105-2649

Dear Mr Knottingham:

    I am writing to request a time frame for a decision on your review of my complaint and Dr. Dave Camel, MD, your file #

Thank you for your consideration in this matter.

Suncerely,

3 Turtle Cove
Oak, PA 18630

COMMONWEALTH OF PENNSYLVANIA
GOVERNOR'S OFFICE OF GENERAL COUNSEL

Sr. Prosecuting Attorney   E-Mail: @state.pa.us

Date: July 16, 2012

3 Turtle Cove

M.D.

You have requested that this office review the decision to close the file against the above-named individual.

After reviewing your request in conjunction with the decision made to close this matter, the matter shall remain closed and this office will not pursue charges against the above-named individual. I can assure you that your complaint has been reviewed by an experienced medical prosecutor and a licensed physician consultant on behalf of the Bureau of Professional and Occupational Affairs, State Board of Medicine. After carefully reviewing your complaint once again, this office has decided not to file formal charges at this time. This matter has been reviewed by numerous attorneys in the Prosecution Division of the Legal Office. The joint opinion of those who have reviewed this case is that there is insufficient evidence to support an allegation that Dr.   deviated from the standard of care regarding your wife.

Further, be advised that the decision not to pursue formal administrative action against Dr.   in this matter constitutes the exercise of prosecutorial discretion in deciding whether or not to press charges against individuals whom it regulates in the exercise of their respective professions in behalf of the public interest. The exercise of such discretion is not properly subject to appeal or judicial review, because such action is not adjudicatory in nature. *See In re Frawley*, 26 Pa. Commw. 517; 364 A.2d 748 (1976). See Wolfe v. Lower Merion School District, 801 A.2d 639 (Pa. Commonwealth Ct. 2002); In Re Frawley, 364 A.2d 748 (Pa. Commonwealth Ct. 1976) Also see Baker v. Penna. Human Relations Commission, 558 A.2d 909 (Pa. Supreme Ct. 1985.)

Thank you for sharing your concerns with the State Board of Medicine. The information you provided will be kept on file and reference to. In addition, the information has been entered into an informational database so that it can be used to determine if there is a pattern of problems with the individual licensees. Although the complaint is being closed, the information will be available for use in the future, if needed.

DEPARTMENT OF STATE/OFFICE OF CHIEF COUNSEL
2601 NORTH 3RD STREET/P.O. BOX 2649//HARRISBURG, PA 17105-2649
PHONE: 717-783-7200/FAX: 717-787-0251/ WWW.DOS.STATE.PA.US

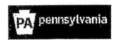

COMMONWEALTH OF PENNSYLVANIA
GOVERNOR'S OFFICE OF GENERAL COUNSEL

Very truly yours,

Sr. Prosecuting Attorney
Department of State

DEPARTMENT OF STATE/OFFICE OF CHIEF COUNSEL
2601 NORTH 3RD STREET/P.O. BOX 2649//HARRISBURG, PA 17105-2649
PHONE: 717-783-7200/FAX: 717-787-0251/ WWW.DOS.STATE.PA.US

BELONGING

Since a little boy growing up in Coney Island, Brooklyn, NY and then becoming a teenager, I've always felt a sense of belonging; my block, my school, "The Big Guys" (our name for the older guys). If you were a good punch ball player, a good baseball player, a good stick ball player, you were picked early when they chose up sides. Since I was a good athlete, I was always picked to play. So I belonged to the Big Guys. Last but not least, I belonged to my mother and father, who gave me the values to keep the rest of my life. I was always loved by them and I returned that love.

When I met Lorraine, fell in love, and married her, after being in the US Navy in World War II, and then twenty-one years in the New York City Police Department, I belonged to my lovely, darling wife Lorraine and she belonged to me. We had a beautiful life, but unfortunately she got dementia with psychosis after a stroke five years previous to her death in 2009. When she was in The Nursing Home of the Angel, after the horrific treatment by a doctor in Crater Memorial Hospital, that caused her death, she died on December 31, 2009 of Aspiration Pneumonia. Having been with her every day and seeing the wonderful care she was given in The Nursing Home of the Angel, I became attached to the facility. They were concerned about me, too. I fell in love with all of them and knew that was where I belonged. Since Lorraine's death three years ago, the staff has become my family. If I can't be with Lorraine now, I want to be nowhere else, but in The Nursing Home of the Angel. As one nurse put it, "You are part of us. No, you belong to us." I love them deeply but I'll always belong to Lorraine for the rest of my life. I'll never belong to anyone else, not ever.

When I die, I'll belong to our own Lord God and be joined with the love of my life, Lorraine, through eternity and those of my family who have passed on. Our souls will be with the great people throughout time who have God's favor. Lorraine and I together forever.

RECEPTION I SAW LORRAINE WORKED
FOR MA BELL

THE ANGEL LORRAINE

CLYDE MAKING A PHONE CALL AT MY HOUSE

ANGEL-TREE AT MY HOUSE

ANGEL-TREE AT MY HOUSE

3 ANGELS SITTING IN MY CHAIR AT HOME

XMAS AT THE HOME OF ANGEL   XMAS AT THE HOME OF THE
                                          ANGEL

HOLLY & CLYDE ON MY COUCH AT HOME

JOSIE & ANGELICA (PUMPKIN) IN MY BED

Yeah, By All Means, Let's Send in the Survey

I am, of course, talking about the survey people get to fill out after being an in-patient and sometimes out-patient at Crater Memorial Hospital. I never complete them, because I know if anything is negative about the stay, they won't acknowledge it. I filled it out two months after my wife died as a result of her stay at Crater Memorial Hospital when her doctor and the PAC Psychiatry went behind my back and gave her medication contra-indicated by the FDA, for her condition. Her treatment by the doctor was abominable. I am including the survey as proof of what I said about no action was taken by the hospital to contact me.

A friend of mine was sick with a broken foot and while I was visiting her, she had another visitor who worked at Crater Memorial Hospital and told me that when something bad comes in, the red flag goes up and the hospital is notified. So I sent it in. What a joke! It says identification is optional, but I wrote my name, address, phone number on the survey and said I would gladly talk to anyone at the hospital about what happened to my wife. Nothing, absolutely no one contacted me. You can put all the comments you want on TV showing how wonderful Crater Memorial Hospital is; I know different. Her stay cost her life at the hands of a doctor.

My wife, who had dementia, died on December 31, 2009, at Little Forks Hospital after being at the Nursing Home of the Angel in Little Forks, PA, of Aspiration Pneumonia. Death by Aspiration Pneumonia is what the FDA stated happens in elderly people with her condition who are given the drug Zyprexa, which was given to her behind my back, after two strokes. Read the survey! My wife died after just two and a half months.

THE SURVEY

10/28/2009

Dear .

Thank you for choosing .   for your health care needs. At
          we want to provide the very best service possible, and we know you expect your care to
be the highest quality available. `

To serve you and meet, our goals, we rely on you to tell us what we do right and what needs
improvement. This means we rely on you to keep us informed.

<u>We need your help.</u>

Please take a moment and fill out our survey, skip any questions that do not apply to you and
return it to us postage-paid. If you recently used any of our other services at `
     , you may receive additional satisfaction surveys. **This survey only relates to your
inpatient stay at** `   Every survey is valuable in helping us evaluate and
enhance our services to you, and we hope you will take a few minutes to complete each survey
you receive.

We appreciate your help.

Thank you.

Sincerely,

President and CEO

INPATIENT SURVEY

We thank you in advance for completing this questionnaire. When you have finished, please mail it in the enclosed envelope.

THIS INPATIENT SURVEY IS FOR MY WIFE. ─OCT?? 2009 TO OCT 26,2009, SHE WAS FORCED TO STAY IN HOSPITHOME AFTER THE HORRIBLE STAY AT

Please rate your visit ending on: 10/26/2009

BACKGROUND QUESTIONS (write in answer or fill in circle (for example ⊙) as appropriate)

1. Patient's first stay here .... O Yes ● No

2. Admitted through the Emergency Department .... O Yes ● No

3. Was your admission unexpected? .... O Yes ● No

4. Did you have a roommate? .... O Yes ● No

5. Were you placed on a special or restricted diet during most of your stay? .... O Yes ● No

6. Did someone explain your extended life support (e.g., living will, advance directives, etc.) options? .... O Yes ● No

7. Did someone give you information about organ donation? .... O Yes ● No

8. Did someone give you information about the Patient's Bill of Rights? .... ● Yes O No

9. Do you have insurance that limits your choice of physician or provider (e.g., HMO or PPO)? .... O Yes ● No   *PLUS MANY SEE BLOW OR DEC.31,09 TT*

10. Main source of payment for hospital stay: (fill in one circle only)
   O Private Insurance
   ● Medicare
   O Medicaid
   O Worker's Compensation
   O Self-Pay

11. Number of days in hospital .... `2` `0` days

12. Compared to others your age, how would you typically describe your health? (fill in one circle only)

very poor	poor	fair	good	very good
O	O	●	O	O

INSTRUCTIONS: Please rate the services you received from our facility. **Fill in the circle** that best describes your experience. If a question does not apply to you, please skip to the next question. Space is provided for you to comment on good or bad things that may have happened to you.

Please use black or blue ink to fill in the circle completely.
Example: ●

A. ADMISSION

	very poor 1	poor 2	fair 3	good 4	very good 5
1. Speed of admission process	●	O	O	O	O
2. Courtesy of the person who admitted you	●	O	O	O	O
3. Rating of pre-admission process (if any)	●	O	O	O	O

Comments (describe good or bad experience): *ADMITTED FROM OUR DR.'S OFFICE AND HE CARED NOTHING ABOUT HER AND HE JUST WANTED HER OUT OF HIS OFFICE, THEN WHY TELL US TO GO TO THO OFFICE & BE ADMITTED FROM THERE?*

continued...

B. ROOM	very poor 1	poor 2	fair 3	good 4	very good 5
1. Pleasantness of room decor	O	O	O	●	O
2. Room cleanliness	O	O	O	●	O
3. Courtesy of the person who cleaned your room	O	O	O	●	O
4. Room temperature	O	O	O	●	O
5. Noise level in and around room	O	O	O	●	O
6. How well things worked (TV, call button, lights, bed, etc.)	O	O	O	●	O

Comments (describe good or bad experience): GOOD

C. MEALS	very poor 1	poor 2	fair 3	good 4	very good 5
1. Temperature of the food (cold foods cold, hot foods hot)	O	O	O	●	O
2. Quality of the food	O	O	O	●	O
3. Courtesy of the person who served your food	O	O	O	●	O

Comments (describe good or bad experience): GOOD - ONLY ATE THE FIRST
5 DAYS AND THEN WAS GIVEN OVERDOSE OF OLANZAPINE
BY THE DOCTOR   AND NEVER ATE AGAIN - SEE
                                                              PHYSICIAN

D. NURSES	very poor 1	poor 2	fair 3	good 4	very good 5
1. Friendliness/courtesy of the nurses	O	O	O	●	O
2. Promptness in responding to the call button	O	O	O	●	O
3. Nurses' attitude toward your requests	O	O	O	●	O
4. Amount of attention paid to your special or personal needs	●	O	O	O	O
5. How well the nurses kept you informed	O	●	O	O	O
6. Skill of the nurses	●	O	O	O	O
7. Nurses' sensitivity and responsiveness to pain you may have experienced in the hospital	●	O	O	O	O

Comments (describe good or bad experience):
INFORMED ONLY WHEN ASKED

E. TESTS AND TREATMENTS	very poor 1	poor 2	fair 3	good 4	very good 5
1. Waiting time for tests or treatments	O	O	O	O	O
2. Concern shown for your comfort during tests or treatments	O	O	O	O	O
3. Explanations about what would happen during tests or treatments	O	O	O	O	O
4. Skill of the person who took your blood (e.g., did it quickly, with minimal pain)	O	O	O	O	O
5. Courtesy of the person who took your blood	O	O	O	O	O
6. Skill of the person who started the IV (e.g., did it quickly, with minimal pain)	O	O	O	O	O
7. Courtesy of the person who started the IV	O	O	O	O	O

Comments (describe good or bad experience):
FAIR TO POOR

419376566

F. SPECIAL SERVICES (IF APPLICABLE)

	very poor 1	poor 2	fair 3	good 4	very good 5
1. Skill of the person who did your physical therapy treatment	O	O	O	O	O
2. Friendliness/courtesy of the person who did your physical therapy treatment	O	O	O	O	O
3. Skill of the Speech Therapist	O	O	O	O	O
4. Friendliness/courtesy of the Speech Therapist	O	O	O	O	O

Comments (describe good or bad experience): DID NOT RECEIVE UNTIL SHE WAS NOT TALKING, EATING, NOT WALKING & THEN NOT TOO RESPONSIVE DUE TO OVERDOSE OF MEDICATION

G. VISITORS AND FAMILY

	very poor 1	poor 2	fair 3	good 4	very good 5
1. Helpfulness of the people at the Information desk	O	O	O	●	O
2. Accommodations and comfort for visitors	O	O	●	O	O
3. Staff attitude toward your visitors	O	O	O	O	O
4. Information given to your family about your condition and treatment	●	O	O	O	O

Comments (describe good or bad experience): I WAS AT HER BEDSIDE THROUGHOUT

H. PHYSICIAN

	very poor 1	poor 2	fair 3	good 4	very good 5
1. Time physician spent with you	●	O	O	O	O
2. Physician's concern for your questions and worries	●	O	O	O	O
3. How well physician kept you informed NOT AT ALL	●	O	O	O	O
4. Friendliness/courtesy of physician	●	O	O	O	O
5. Skill of physician	●	O	O	O	O
6. Physician's sensitivity and responsiveness to pain you may have experienced in the hospital	●	O	O	O	O

Comments (describe good or bad experience): TERRIBLE - HE KEPT AWAY EXCEPT TO TRY TO GET RID OF HER! HE NEVER ONCE CONSULTED NO REGARDING MEDICATION AND HE GAVE HER THE OVERDOSE 2 DAYS BEFORE WE WERE SUPPOSE TO LEAVE AND SHE SLEPT 33 HOURS AND NEVER TALKED AGAIN, NEVER WALKED AGAIN, NEVER ATE AGAIN NEVER SWALLOWED AGAIN THAT WAS

I. DISCHARGE

	very poor 1	poor 2	fair 3	good 4	very good 5
1. Extent to which you felt ready to be discharged	O	O	O	O	O
2. Speed of discharge process after you were told you could go home	●	O	O	O	O
3. Instructions given about how to care for yourself at home	●	O	O	O	O
4. Help with arranging home care services (if needed)	O	O	O	O	O

Comments (describe good or bad experience): WE HAD TO PUT HER IN A NURSING HOME AFTER WHAT DID TO HE. HE KEPT US WAITING FOR OVER 3 HRS AND THEN SENT HIS PARTNER BECAUSE HE DOESN'T FIRE ME OR MY WIFE

BECAUSE OF WHAT HE HAD DONE.
YOU GOT GIVE A DOUBLE DOSE OF PSYCHOTIC MED TO A 76 YR OLD WOMAN WITH MEMORY PROBLEMS AND DEMENTIA! BUT   DID!

continued...

- 93 -

J. PERSONAL ISSUES

	very poor 1	poor 2	fair 3	good 4	very good 5
1. Staff concern for your privacy	O	O	O	O	O
2. Staff sensitivity to the inconvenience that health problems and hospitalization can cause	O	O	O	O	O
3. How well your pain was controlled	O	O	O	O	O
4. Degree to which hospital staff addressed your emotional/spiritual needs	O	O	O	O	O
5. Response to concerns/complaints made during your stay	O	O	O	O	O
6. Staff effort to include you in decisions about your treatment	O	O	O	O	O
7. Degree of safety you felt in our center	●	O	O	O	O

Comments (describe good or bad experience): MADE HER
I DID NOT FEEL SAFE FOR HER AFTER - A ZOMBIE AND THEN STARTED A SERIES OF LIES TO GET
OUT FROM UNDER BY COVERING HIS MISTAKE.

K. OVERALL ASSESSMENT

	very poor 1	poor 2	fair 3	good 4	very good 5
1. Overall cheerfulness of the hospital	●	O	O	O	O
2. How well staff worked together to care for you	●	O	O	O	O
3. Likelihood of your recommending this hospital to others	●	O	O	O	O
4. Overall rating of care given at hospital	●	O	O	O	O

Comments (describe good or bad experience): HORRIBLE

* MY WIFE DIED ON DEC 31, 2007 AT
LAYED THE GROUNDWORK FOR HER STROKE AT _____ FOLLOWED
BY OXYGEN DROP, PNEUMONIA AND THEN WHEN WE MOVED HER
TO THE NURSING HOME IN _____ ANOTHER STROKE
HIS OVERDOSE OF PSYCHOTIC MEDICATION STARTED HER DOWNHILL - SURVEY DONE BY HUSBAND

Patient's Name: (optional) _____

Telephone Number: (optional) 570- CELL # 570-

INSTEAD OF 2 DAYS AT _____ TURNED INTO
20 DAYS, WE COULD HAVE GONE HOME BUT DR
MADE SURE WE WERE THERE LONGER WITH HIS OVERDOSE TO MY WIFE.

WE WALKED INTO THE HOSP. SHE WAS A FUNCTIONING HUMAN
BEING AND SHE WAS CARRIED OUT AND TILL THE DAY SHE
DIED SHE COULDN'T WALK, TALK, SWALLOW, EAT AND WAS
IN A VEGETATION STATE BECAUSE OF THE MEDICATION SHE
WAS GIVEN WITHOUT MY KNOWLEDGE BY DR.

I'LL BE HAPPY TO ANSWER ANY QUESTIONS YOU
HAVE IN THIS MATTER. THERE'S MANY MORE THINGS YOU
SHOULD KNOW OF. CONDUCT -
AND HER STAY AT

PRESS·GANEY®

419376566

NO POSTAGE
NECESSARY
IF MAILED
IN THE
UNITED STATES

BUSINESS REPLY MAIL

FIRST-CLASS MAIL   PERMIT NO. 2366   SOUTH BEND IN

POSTAGE WILL BE PAID BY ADDRESSEE

SURVEY PROCESSING DEPARTMENT
PRESS GANEY
PO BOX 7006.
SOUTH BEND IN 46699-0468

Please return ONLY THE SURVEY in this business reply envelope to the Survey Processing Center. Do not include billing or other statements, checks, or other non-survey materials. Thank You.

SENT . 2-8-10

```
               ~~~~~~~~~~~~~~
                 ~~~~~~~~
               4134870301 -0096
02/06/2010     (570)421-3310     10:12:26 AM
               ---------------------------------
                   Sales Receipt
Product          Sale  Unit         Final
Description        Qty Price         Price

SOUTH BEND IN 46699                  $0.44
Zone-4 First-Class
Letter
0.60 oz.
Return Rcpt (Green Card)             $2.30
Certified                            $2.80
Label #:       70082610000219115698
                                   =========
Issue PVI:                           $5.54

2009 Forever      1    $8.80         $8.80
Stamp PSA
Dbl-Sd Bklt

Total:                              $14.34

Paid by:
Cash                                $20.34
Change Due:                         -$6.00

Order stamps at USPS.com/shop or call
1-800-Stamp24.  Go to USPS.com/clicknship
to print shipping labels with postage.
For other information call 1-800-ASK-USPS.
*******************************************
Get your mail when and where you want it
with a secure Post Office Box. Sign up for
a box online at usps.com/poboxes.
*******************************************
*******************************************

Bill#: 1000401797385
Clerk: 07

All sales final on stamps and postage
Refunds for guaranteed services only
Thank you for your business
*******************************************
*******************************************
       HELP US SERVE YOU BETTER

Go to: https://postalexperience.com/Pos

   TELL US ABOUT YOUR RECENT
        POSTAL EXPERIENCE

     YOUR OPINION COUNTS
*******************************************
*******************************************


         Customer Copy
```

U.S. Postal Service
CERTIFIED MAIL RECEIPT
(Domestic Mail Only; No Insurance Coverage Provided)

OFFICIAL USE

Postage	$	$2.20	0301 07
Certified Fee		$2.80	
Return Receipt Fee (Endorsement Required)		$2.30	
Restricted Delivery Fee (Endorsement Required)		$0.00	
Total Postage & Fees	$		

Sent To

Street, Apt. No.; or PO Box No.

City, State, ZIP+4

7008 2810 0002 1911 5698

SENDER: COMPLETE THIS SECTION

- Complete items 1, 2, and 3. Also complete item 4 if Restricted Delivery is desired.
- Print your name and address on the reverse so that we can return the card to you.
- Attach this card to the back of the mailpiece, or on the front if space permits.

1. Article Addressed to:

SURVEY PROCESSING DEPT
PRESS GARVEY
P.O. BOX 7006
SOUTH BEND IN
46699-0866

2. Article Number
(Transfer from service label)
7008 2810 0002 1911 5698

PS Form 3811, February 2004   Domestic Return Receipt

COMPLETE THIS SECTION ON DELIVERY

A. Signature
X _____ □ Agent □ Addressee

B. Received by (Printed Name)   C. Date of Delivery
                                2/12/10

D. Is delivery address different from item 1? □ Yes
   If YES, enter delivery address below: □ No

3. Service Type
   ☒ Certified Mail   □ Express Mail
   □ Registered   □ Return Receipt for Merchandise
   □ Insured Mail   □ C.O.D.

4. Restricted Delivery? (Extra Fee)   □ Yes

WHERE IS LORRAINE AND THE CHRISTMAS TREES?

The stores are loaded with Christmas trees and "stuff" but where are they in the place I call the house? It is not a home. Home is where Lorraine and I lived. She designed it and we had it built. We had 1.5 acres of land, a private 400 foot road, and 8 very spacious rooms one of which was the Christmas room with five trees in it. They, as well as all the trees, remained there all year long and were never taken down. Lorraine loved Christmas. One tree was covered with all Garfield ornaments, one with ornaments from Poland and Germany, one with angel ornaments, one with cat ornaments, and one with gold and silver mixtures. There are trees all over the house and one big monster tree with all gold ornaments in the living room.

After Lorraine's death I couldn't stand to see everything that we built and in this beautiful house. I came to the decision to let others enjoy what we had and selectively gave things away so others hoping they would experience the enjoyment we did. Eventually I moved into a gated community where I wouldn't have to mow or plow. I kept things that were dear to both of us, including our bedroom set, where I now sleep on her side. I took a five foot Christmas tree and adorned it with the angel ornaments from the big angel tree and it sits on the living room floor. Our pictures are all framed 8" x 10" and sit on the table in front of the couch. There is a picture of our white-water rafting in Colorado, one of us on the Mendenhall Glacier in Juneau, Alaska, those of a few close friends and the Cohen Serenity Garden with an angel statue perched on a hill. I had built this garden in Lorraine's honor at the The Nursing Home of the Angel in Little Forks, PA. That was the place I had to bring Lorraine to hopefully get well and where she died on December 31, 2009 of Aspiration Pneumonia at Little Forks, PA Hospital. According to the FDA, Aspiration Pneumonia is one of the two most common causes of death due to using Zyprexa in elderly people with dementia and psychosis and why the FDA "black box warning" clearly contraindicates it for a patient like Lorraine. Dr. Camel gave it to her any way behind my back. The nursing center will be addressed in another chapter. I go to the garden regularly and I also am an official volunteer there.

Anyway, I live in this townhouse alone and think about nothing else except her and how to get justice for her. I eventually sold the house and my life is centered about making the Doctor accountable and responsible for her death. I took no money for anything. I only ever wanted the doctor to be accountable and punished for his actions. I did not sue the doctor in Civil Court for money.

THE LONG, LONG WAIT

Let me bring you to the agency that held me hostage in my quest for justice for my wife. The complaint was made to the Bureau of Professional and Occupational Affairs at the Department of State. As noted, after contacting the Legal Bureau on December 10, 2010, I began speaking to Attorney Clark Wayne on January 4, 2011 and he said to call him again on February 4, 2011. Kindly refer to "First contact with the Legal Bureau" and "Subsequent Conversations with Attorney Clark Wayne" which follows this chapter. They are very important especially from June 21, 2011 to the end and the ensuing "Timeline."

Justice is all I ever wanted for my wife since Dr. Camel did what he did to her with the Zyprexa medication at Crater Memorial Hospital from October 7, 2009 to October 11, 2009.

Lorraine wasn't some crazed psycho with a machete. She was a functional woman with dementia and psychosis and completely harmless, talking to herself. After Dr. Camel administered the Zyprexa, no follow-up care, and experiencing a stroke, I then took her to The Nursing Home of the Angel in Little Forks, PA. There she suffered from another stroke and several bouts with pneumonia and finally passed away on December 31, 2009 of Aspiration Pneumonia.

I want him to be responsible for her death, which would be justice. I tried speaking to five lawyers who refused the case. I then took the Department of State route and the following sequence of events took place. I hired a nurse who worked for a pharmaceutical company in New Jersey. Her job was to take and read the pages of my wife's medical record.

With a Power of Attorney, I went to the Patients Records Office at Crater Memorial Hospital and got my wife's medical records. This was after she was at the nursing home but before her death. I arranged for the nurse to review my wife's medical records and make a report of her findings. She found that Dr. Camel put a DNR on her chart. A RN took verbal orders over the phone and signed her name; he overdosed my wife on a medication called Zyprexa, with Black Box warnings not to give it to elderly people with dementia and psychosis, because they die from it. The leading causes of death are Cardio Vascular and Aspiration Pneumonia. With this information, I filed an Ethical Complaint against Dr. Camel with the Bureau of Professional and Occupational Affairs at the Department of State.

Why Was My Case against Dr. Camel Closed

Attorney Clark Wayne told me the following after telling me they were closing the case against Dr. Camel.

1. The outside expert said there was "no deviation of standard" care of my wife. I replied, "So, it is OK for a doctor to put DNR on my wife without consultation and behind my back. He could also give her Zyprexa even though the FDA said it was not approved for her condition."

2. The outside expert said "Olanzapine"/Zyprexa is used for different patients. I said, "Yes, but not for elderly people with dementia and psychosis because they die from it. And my wife <u>did die</u> from all the dosing given to her."

3. He said Dr. Camel told the outside expert that Marjorie Nelson, PAC Psychiatry, initiated the ordering of Zyprexa and he didn't know what to do so he asked other doctors. Attorney Wayne had asked the outside doctor if he ever spoke to Dr. Camel and he said "No." So how did he know of the conversation with Dr. Camel and Marjorie Nelson? The outside expert doctor lied. Nowhere in her medical records is there an indication of such a conversation.

4. I asked Attorney Wayne if the outside doctor came to the office to read my wife's paper and he answered that the records were sent to him. I then asked him, "why not? You were given $5000 to read Lorraine's records. Why couldn't he have gone to the office directly and read them?" Now my wife's records were

compromised. He lied about talking to Dr. Camel, so now Dr. Camel has access to her records and he was ripe for the sell-out.

5. The outside doctor told Attorney Wayne he turned in five pages. For all anyone knows, Dr. Camel could have written them for him.

6. Isn't it odd that the in-house doctor took almost nine months to read her records and said the case had merit and to move on. Yet the outside doctor only took two months and said no case and he refused to testify against Dr. Camel. So after nine months of waiting, I was sold out and given no reason! And Dr. Camel is not charged and possibly buys himself out and there is certainly a buy-out!

I wrote and called the FDA, the Attorney General, Ombudsman for the FDA, and (as advised by the Attorney General's office) wrote the Commissioner of the Bureau of Professional and Occupational Affairs – Prosecutorial Division. I wrote to Commissioner Sally Falstaff, the two letters which are provided. I then heard from her Chief Counsel Gerald Berry who notified me that the case is re-opened for re-review as per Commissioner Falstaff. Attorney Alex Nottingham will do the reading. Eight and a half months later, I received a letter from Attorney Nottingham that "because of insufficient evidence, Dr. Camel would not be charged and the case is closed." Twice shut down. I had and have such overwhelming evidence against Dr. Camel. I can't and won't believe the case was read at all. They wanted enough time to pass to make it look like they did. During that eight and a half month period, I called Attorney Nottingham two times and wrote him one note to check on the status of the case and he ignored both the calls and the note. All the correspondence is included in the book.

I must at this time tell you of my conversation with the FDA Ombudsman. She said, "The FDA has no involvement in regulating physicians. Physicians are regulated by the State Board of Medicine in Pennsylvania." The PA Attorney General does not prosecute licensed doctors either. I called them and they asked for my wife's records. I sent them along with my complaint. They read the records for four days then called me back and spoke to me and did nothing. Just proving they do nothing about complaints either. Who does?

I told the Ombudsman from the FDA that they should disband if they do not enforce their own edicts.

I told the agent from the Attorney General's office that they are the largest law agency in the State of Pennsylvania and a doctor violates a mandate of the FDA, and uses the medication anyway and it killed my wife and nothing is done. Nobody enforces anything and people die.

THE CRIME OF THE 21ST CENTURY

The crime of the 21st century was a letter to me dated July 16, 2012 from Senior Prosecuting Attorney Alex Nottingham, Department of State, advising me that the review of my closed case against Dr. Dave Camel "shall remain closed."

This decision makes the crime of the 21st Century because it is a travesty of justice and for the second time the state has closed the door of justice for my wife on an air tight case, that is anyone reading it would say, "GUILTY" and not "close the case." A deal was obviously made. They never read the case but just placated me by saying they would and were just waiting for me to die or just give up and saw fit to make me wait eight and a half months and then send me a letter saying "Insufficient Evidence." The first time they closed the case after 9 months with no reason. Any man who did to my wife with the Zyprexa that Dr. Camel used on her and caused her death, then gets off with no charge of negligence and no prosecution, should have his license taken away from him for gross negligence. The person or persons responsible for aiding and abetting him, should also lose their jobs and be ashamed and looked down upon for the rest of their lives for their crime along with Dr. Camel. They should have to wear a picture around their necks of my wife as she looked when she was killed being unable to walk, talk, unable to eat or swallow, with a peg in her stomach for liquid food and last but not least she could not see! What heroes, the doctor and his pals are, aren't they! I'm not finished yet. Now I'll solve the crime that led to the crime of the 21st Century. Dr. Camel and his cohort Marjorie Nelson PAC Psychiatry were feeding my wife Zyprexa from the first day in the hospital. Her medical records show this to be true. In meetings with neurology & psychiatry under the supervision of Dr. Camel that first time in the hospital I told them I didn't want my wife doped up or made a zombie. The only medication is to be Exelon patch for her memory. They agreed and lied and gave her Zyprexa and a DNR without discussion with me (see the complaint) from that first day Dr. Camel kept after me telling me that she had terminal dementia repeating that over and over to me and I asked him if he's building a cause of death and he kept away from me from then on. Lorraine was eating and kept to herself and went to the bathroom. She was very quiet. She began to eat less and less. Five days later she was overdosed with 10mg of Zyprexa after being given 5mg in the daytime. I had told Dr. Camel I was taking her home with assistance that afternoon and he overdosed her that evening. I was with her everyday till after supper. The overdose was on Sunday evening and she slept for 33 hours and had a stroke during that time. I asked the nurse if she was on anything and who ordered it. She said 10mg of Zyprexa and Dr. Camel ordered it. I then found out what happened. When she awoke she could not walk, talk, eat, swallow, or see. His plan didn't work: she was supposed to die and she didn't and he knew I would never have her cut in an autopsy and he could blame the death on her dementia. The IV pole was still empty. He waited for her to die, 2 ½ months later she died from Aspiration Pneumonia caused by the Zyprexa.

From Crater Memorial Hospital I had to place her in the Nursing Home of the Angel where she had a second stroke. She died at Little Forks Hospital in Little Forks. Before she died I got her medical records with a Power of Attorney and everything was clear what happened at Crater Memorial Hospital in Cedar, PA. Her records revealed the dosage of Zyprexa and how I was thinking did they manage to give her the Zyprexa in the daytime, simple: they mashed the pill and put it in her chocolate pudding (noted in the nurses notes) It also noted Dr. Camels admission of giving her the overdose. The medical records appear at the end of the book. At the Nursing Home of the Angel she got excellent medical treatment and superb rehab but Dr. Camel's Zyprexa was too much for her and she passed away on December 31, 2009. I shouldn't say passed away, I should say killed. It's all there in her records! Why doesn't somebody honest read them? Especially where the FDA says Zyprexa is not to be given to elderly people with psychosis because they die from it. And my wife DID!

COMMEMORATIVE ACTIVITES

Since Lorraine's passing my main focus has been the Nursing Home of the Angel. The garden that was dedicated to Lorraine has been a popular attraction and an integral part of the home itself. I covered that in the chapter entitled "Lorraine's Death".

Following Lorraine's death I set up the Lorraine Cohen Memorial Fund checking account in which I make donations to several charities in her honor. I made a large monetary contribution to her Methodist church. After her stroke in 1998 Lorraine had 50 pairs of brand new shoes which was donated to the church along with the donation for the less fortunate. I also buy turkeys every holiday to help with feeding the homeless.

Currently I am assisting with tuition payments for Selena Patel, a brilliant young Student who is attending medical school in Philadelphia P.A. with an interest in Dementia & Alzheimer diseases. She is half way through her education and is a straight A student. I keep hoping she will be part of a group to find a cure for the dementia that ravaged my wife's brain. She didn't die from Dementia, but at the hands of Dr. Camel at Crater Memorial Hospital from Aspiration Pneumonia.

Another charity I contribute to is Breast Cancer Awareness, and 5k run was in her name. One 5-k run was in her honor by Unico Hazleton Bell Italia Festival in Hazleton, PA. The name unico is the Italian word for unique, one of a kind. They were gracious by having a picture of my wife on the tee shirts of the runners to let everyone know who is being honored. I'm a contributor every year since that first run in 2011. Last year Lorraine's picture on a coffee mug was sent to me for my contribution. All contributions go to the needy, the poor and the homeless, and I'm also honoring my mother.

As a child growing up my mother always used to tell me "You my son are from a poor working class family, so if you ever have a few extra dollars to spare share it with other poor working class people as you have known their troubles." Lorraine also had the same beliefs so all contributions are to those less fortunate in honor of my wife and in memory of my mother.

PEOPLE'S THOUGHTS OF LORRAINE

Lorraine didn't have too many close friends here because we were always on the go. I was teaching at the university level and if you know college life there is a lot of time off. You have Christmas, Spring Break, summer, after the summer before the fall Semester starts and Thanksgiving time. There are periods when you can get away for a few days, a week, etc. Due to the nature of the job we kept to ourselves and Lorraine didn't work so we took off at any time. We both loved to travel so it was no hardship for us to get in the car and go on the short hops. Her best friend was still in Richmond and we visit her often.

I spoke to men and women we were friendly with, shopkeepers we frequented, and neighbors. One story comes to mind immediately. This deals with her kindness and generosity. We were visiting one Richmond, VA friend of hers she went to school with and it was Valentine's Day. Lorraine wanted to stop in a store to get some candy to bring to her and she noticed a young girl about 12 years of age holding a box of candy under her coat. Lorraine went right over to the girl and said "Give me the candy you have under your coat." The girl didn't fight about it she just gave it up. Lorraine also told the girl to stay put and don't run out. And went to the counter, paid for the box of candy and brought it to the young girl and gave it to her. The girl said it was for her mother and hugged Lorraine, said thank you and left the store. The owner came over to us and said he had seen the girl take the candy and hasn't seen that kindness and generosity in a long time and offered a free box of candy and Lorraine paid for another box of candy for her friend and we left the store. That was an example of kindness and generosity that my beautiful wife had. She had a beautiful heart and that was my darling. My pride and joy. Some years have passed since the incident. We returned to

Richmond, VA and stopped at that same candy store and lo and behold that young girl is now a young woman and a sales lady in the store. She spotted Lorraine, ran to her, hugged her and said "I'll never forget you. I love you" the owner was still there too.

A friend of ours loved her southern accent. It was no put on, it was genuine like my Brooklyn accent. I'm proud of the way I speak. It is pure Brooklyn and not New York. There is a difference, my baby is proud of her accent too. She has been called kind, affectionate and loving by someone else we know. She never hurt a soul said another. Some people mention and admire her posture. She walks with no bending over. Her legs are like steel. She took pride in flexing her thighs and says touch them. The people do say they're amazed at her. As an example when she was in rehab at the Nursing Home of the Angel, the staff used to marvel when her legs were being worked on. Working one at a time her legs were absolutely perpendicular to the ground, straight as an arrow. One amazement after another.

When we were dancing anywhere people came up to us and say Lorraine had a passion for the dance. She always got compliments. I was so proud of her.

We have a Chinese friend who has a take-out restaurant who runs it with her husband and son. She loves American food and used to come to our house and I would cook for her and Lorraine. Lorraine bought her a ring with Chinese inscriptions on the outside meaning health and prosperity. She loved Lorraine and came often to the house. She was very hospitable when people came into the house. They remember that for a long time and remark to that effect. Some others say you could never get in a fight with her she refused to make herself look foolish or mad. She had no temper and always had herself under control.

When she got the Dementia we did a lot of driving and stopped every day at Turkey Hill on route 611 and while I was inside getting some food for us to eat in the car the girl at the register near the window used to watch for Lorraine if she opened the car door and tried to get out of the car. In fact all the girls used to watch for her because they loved her courage and if she did try they would alert me and I would go put her back in the car. Lorraine was always nice to the girls who always tried to help her.

Another trait of her was being courteous to people. There was very little anger in her. Most of the people I asked said she was a sweet person with no axe to grind against anyone. She lived and let live. Other people said it was a pleasure being around her. Others said she was a very intelligent woman and many of her friends would urge her to go on Jeopardy. She was a good athlete in school and there were those (and I concur) who said she was a terrific tennis player. All the comments about her were positive. She was a superb human being who loved life. I'm lucky to have had someone as my dear wife and we were blessed in our relationship. Ours was a great love. Just ask anybody.

WHERE IS THE JUSTICE FOR LORRAINE

The decision to close the case a second time against Dr. Camel is totally unacceptable to me. I had an air-tight case against him and nothing of the truth prevailed and nothing manifested from all the documentation. I was with my wife every morning at 7:00 am until after she ate supper.

My wife's medical records obtained from Crater Memorial Hospital clearly state that a DNR code was put on her chart the first day she was admitted to the hospital on a verbal order without discussion with me. I want to know why a DNR code was ordered when all I did was bring her to the hospital, under her own power, to be checked out. Lorraine had stopped eating and I wanted to be sure she was okay. There was no dire emergency present. The Zyprexa was given to my wife the first day, without my consultation and behind my back by Marjorie Nelson PAC Psychiatry. The Zyprexa was not approved by the FDA for my wife's condition, dementia with psychosis, because elderly people with that condition who are given that medication die from it. She died from "Aspiration Pneumonia" at Little Forks Hospital on December 31, 2009 from the medication given to her on the first day by Dr. Camel and Marjorie Nelson, unbeknownst to me. Obviously, if they had told me their plans than everything they were doing would come to an immediate stop by me. In the initial meeting with Neurology and Marjorie Nelson, under the direction of Dr. Camel, I told them in no uncertain terms that I didn't want her doped up or made into a zombie. I only wanted her on the Exelon patch for her memory. They agreed to this but did not hold to it; and consequently she died.

Dr. Camel has to be made accountable and responsible for what he did to my wife as well as Marjorie Nelson PAC Psychiatry in the

Behavioral Health unit, now with an office across the street from Crater Memorial Hospital; a reward for her part in the death of my wife or for silence.

I have a great deal of respect for Commissioner Sally Falstaff but for the second time overwhelming evidence against Dr. Camel has been overlooked or ignored or both, in a read of the case against him.

Everyone involved in this deal to escape prosecution whether it be money, closing one of his practices or a part of both, have become accessories after the fact to her death.

Why did Attorney Nottingham refuse to talk to me when I called him two times and wrote him a note once to find out the status of the read? I want to believe there will eventually be someone brave enough to desert the ship of conspiracy, and come forth to tell everything. We all know something happened and most know the reason my file was closed.

Dr. Camel, Marjorie Nelson, the "expert" outside doctor, the group of consultants mentioned by Attorney Nottingham sold me out by saying there was insufficient evidence to charge Dr. Camel and earlier said there was no deviation from standard care. Anyone else who failed to or chose not to charge him or prosecute him will eventually be challenged in the court of public opinion. I can't and won't ever stop trying to get justice for my harmless and helpless wife and will use every option open to me to do this. This I swear on my now "God's Angel" wife, Lorraine.

This is also an indictment of the doctors who run Health Care Systems in general and those doctors, in particular, who have seen fit to use medication contrary to FDA recommendations. The FDA did not approve Zyprexa in cases of elderly with dementia and psychosis because studies revealed it results in death. However, doctors, like Dr. Camel, use it anyway without fear of legal ramifications knowing full well that fellow doctors and other medical staff will protect them when they are "in trouble before a board of inquiry."

First and foremost, I did not bring my wife into the hospital for placement in a skilled nursing facility which is another lie Dr. Camel alludes to in his group that includes Margaret Tubb, the caseworker. I brought Lorraine in to the ER to be checked out because she stopped eating and I was concerned for her health. The caseworker Margaret

Tubb spread his lies by repeating what he told her. To witch, she said my wife occasionally hit me, which simply wasn't true. Margaret Tubb started to push me to place Lorraine in a nursing home. That was also part of Camel's plan since at one point, several years prior, during one of my own appointments he told the nurse to give me some addresses and phone numbers of nursing homes and I said "No, what are you doing?" and he said "Better now than later." I yelled "No", I didn't want any of it and ran out of the office. Lorraine was never a burden to me and I always took care of her.

On Sunday October 11, 2009, I told him I was taking Lorraine home with assistance and he said wait till Tuesday when he would discharge her in the P.M. That night he overdosed her. He wasn't about to let her go home alive. I still did not know at the time he was giving her Zyprexa. What followed was the most horrific time of both Lorraine's life and my own. She has a stroke from medication, slept over 33 hours, had to have oxygen at ICU, had a PEG tube put into her stomach to be fed over Camel's objections. After that, I had no choice but to place her in a nursing center in Little Forks where she died December 31, 2009 from the Zyprexa he had administered while in Crater Memorial Hospital. Zyprexa clearly was contraindicated by the FDA for elderly people with dementia and psychosis because they die from it. God gave me time to continue my mission of getting Dr. Camel. Only the Lord determines who lives or dies not a rogue doctor! The story will be covered in another chapter; the search for justice and the truth.

THE ADMISSION IN CAMEL's OWN WRITING HE GAVE HER AN OVERDOSE OF 10mg "just a bit overly sedated" he says. "Perhaps it is not only the <u>one</u> 10mg she had but a cumulative dose since hospitalization. He also gave her 5mg in the afternoon. What would you do? He and his "partner" did her in! When she awoke after over 33 hours, she couldn't walk, talk, eat, swallow or see!! That was some overdose.

COUNTING MY BLESSINGS

I thank God for the wonderful life he gave me. I bless my dear mother and father who came to America as poor Russian Immigrants to escape persecution and made a life for themselves. They had the wisdom to instill in me what the right and wrong thing to do the important action is to help others. That is and has been my main focus. I've been aware of the work ethic since I was nine years old. Nothing comes easy. You don't take the easy way out by stealing or maneuvering or doing anything illegal. Work is the easy way out. Your conscience will be clear and your mind at ease. I learned well. My father was a Kohein who were priests thousands of years ago and the kohanim lineage continues today. So I have his blood in me and it keeps me straight and blessed and proud that I come from a line of Jewish priests.

As I said before I had a good life. I did well in school; I am a world war II Navy Veteran, after the war I became a police officer in the City of New York. While a police officer I attended John Jay College of Criminal Justice and attained a Bachelor of Science in Police Science and a Masters of Public Administration. When I retired in 1973, I taught at the University for 25 years and retired in August 1997. I also had a villa in Southern Spain after meeting and marrying the love of my life: Lorraine on August 29, 1974. we met November 25, 1972 and always considered our wedding anniversary, along with our legal anniversary. The Lord God blessed both of us being so much in love. We both enjoyed traveling so we did. We just about saw the world, Europe, Asia, 15 cruises, whitewater rafting on the Colorado River in Durango, Colorado. I have chapters of our travels in the book.

The blessings of both received enriched both of our lives. I absolutely loved taking care that she had anything she wanted or needed. Yes, I spoiled her, but she did the same for me. We took care of each other. We needed, wanted, and had each other. Nothing mattered as long as we were together. There was nothing as she or me it was always us. I cry every day for my blessed angel.

The purpose of the book is to get her story and my story out so people will be on extra guard when they take a loved one to a hospital. I did and the doctors still killed her. The book tells us why and how and by whom she was murdered. She passed away December 31, 2009 by Aspiration Pneumonia.

LORRAINE SPEAKS

On October 11, 2009 after the double overdose of Zyprexa, 10mg at 22:02 hrs and 5mg at 11:12am a total of 15mg for the day by Dr. Camel of Crater Memorial Hospital she slept for 33 hours and had a stroke according to a timeline of Dr. Manual Costas, neurologist. I was there on Monday October 12, 2009 at 7am till she opened her eyes about 7am October 13, 2009. I called for Dr. Camel all day Monday and Tuesday. He finally Tuesday evening at 7pm. I asked the nurse "What was she on?" and she said Zyprexa 10mgs an anti-psychotic drug. I asked her who ordered it and she said Dr. Camel. When she awoke for a short time she couldn't walk, talk, eat, swallow or see. That's what he did to my wife.

She didn't speak until she was at The Nursing Home of the Angel. As with people with Dementia, the wires in the brain are scrambled and sometimes they connect and you have the ability to speak. For how long no one knows. I know where and when she spoke and what she said. I was going to share it with no one because she is mine and there are not many people around here and in Morganville who cared if she lived or died. The caring ones worked at the Nursing Home of the Angel. Against my better judgment I'll do it and maybe it will bring some shame to their souls if they have any.

Thursday October 29, 2009

The Nursing Home of the Angel – Wendy, one of the nurses is doing some oral cleaning and brushes Lorraine's hair and says "Conrad is on his way to see you." Lorraine says "good" then Wendy "Conrad is a good man" and Lorraine said "I know"

Monday November 2, 2009

The Nursing Home of the Angel- Lorraine has a stroke and is taken to Little Forks Hospital they took photos of the brain and think they see blood on the brain. They then transfer her to Elm Street Hospital, take photos of her brain (they have neurosurgeons) and say it is residue from the stroke and put her in I.C.U.

Friday November 6, 2009

Elm Street Hospital – I come to see Lorraine early November 6, 2009 Friday naturally I'm always there or anywhere she is until late at night and then leave for home or in many case sleep there. They tell me in ICU she's in a different room because in the afternoon she will be going back to the nursing home. I go to the room they have moved her to and there is another bed with a woman in it and her husband in a chair and she asked me "who is Conrad?" and I said "That's me I'm her husband. Why?" The woman said "She was calling you all night to help her. And who is Judy she called her too for help but only for a very short time for her mother"

Wednesday November 18, 2009

The Nursing Home of the Angel – I told you everything about physical therapy and about Scott alias Peter Pan this day in therapy Lorraine stood up twice and she was lying down and Scott was working on her legs and her neck and then he said "O.K. Lorraine you stood up 2 times, do you want to try for three?" And she said to him "No, I'm tired."

December 31, 2009

Little Forks Hospital – Lorraine was in the hospital since December 19, 2009 with Pneumonia. I had been sleeping at the hospital almost every day on Wednesday December 30, 2009 I decided to go home and shower and get a good night sleep and go to the hospital nice and early. I left about 4 pm and was soon showered and in my pajamas and in the chair watching TV, and watched the weather and lo and behold, the forecast for Thursday was the next am was at 6am up in Cedar and 7am snow at the nursing home. I jumped up and said I had to get back to the hospital. I dressed real quick and went back to the hospital. They said I still could sleep in the room, I said No, You've put a woman in with my wife and it wouldn't be right, I'll sleep in the waiting room. I went to the waiting room and came out every half hour to check on my love. That went on all night and at 6am I came into her room and a couple of nurses were suctioning her and I came alongside the bed and held her hand tight. I then noticed a little yellow stuff in the corner of her eye and tried to get it off with my finger. She then shouted "Ow my eye". I said I'm sorry and kissed her eye. Then a nurse came in to check her vitals and I said "you don't have to worry about her oxygen, it's usually 94-97 and it was 40". I said "check again" and it was 40 again. They called "stat" and put me out of the room and help came from all over. About 15 minutes to a half hour later they came out and she had a pipe in her mouth. I caught up with her and held her hand and went in the elevator to ICU and waited outside. A nurse came out and I signed for a chest tube. My wife Lorraine died at 10:55 am from Aspiration Pneumonia.

For more information on her death see the chapter "Lorraine's Death"

Lorraine's Death

I brought her to Crater Memorial Hospital October 7, 2009. What needs to be addressed first is that my wife Lorraine walked into Crater Memorial Hospital under her own power. She wasn't brought by ambulance on a stretcher. She was never bed-ridden because I saw to it that she gets out every day; not lying in bed. She enjoyed riding in the car anywhere from three or four to seven hours a day. We rode up and down Route 509, Route 311 and down to Wegman's for a slice of pizza. She loved being out so much, she hated to come home. She was never a burden to me, not ever. As Dr. Camel said when I brought her in for her vitals, "She's stronger than anyone I knew with a strong heart and always good numbers." He was our family doctor and then decides she's not worth keeping alive anymore. He was our family doctor since 1997 so he knew what to do to get rid of her. It was not his call. Only God gets to decide who lives or dies, not him. It is well-documented by her medical records that he put DNR on her the first day she was there and gave her Zyprexa on that first day also. The Zyprexa is not approved for her condition. It kills elderly people. The cause of her death was aspiration pneumonia caused by the Zyprexa.

I brought her to the hospital because she had stopped eating and I was afraid for her health. I just wanted her checked out. The first day I met with Psychiatry and Neurology under the direction of Dr. Camel and they agreed to my demand that under no circumstance will she be overdosed or made a zombie with any medicine. The only medication was to be an Exelon patch for memory. They agreed. The lies started the first day when they gave her Zyprexa and put her on DNR. Again, this is documented and everything they did was behind my back. They never ever had a discussion with me about either!! Or anything for that matter.

The medications are in the complaint and clearly show October 7, 8, 9, 10 and 11 that 52.5 mg of Zyprexa were given to her. I saw Dr. Camel on October 11 and told him I was taking her home with assistance. He said that I should wait until Tuesday and then he would discharge her in the afternoon. That evening he overdosed her with 10 mg after 5 mg in the afternoon. Then she slept for thirty-three hours. The time line given to me by Dr. Costas was October 11 to October 15. When she awoke, she had become a cripple not being able to walk, talk, eat, swallow or see. Then she developed pneumonia and he was against me having a PEG (Percutaneous endoscopic gastrostomy) tube placed into her stomach, otherwise she would die. He said, "It was not humane." I said, "You did it! You gave her the overdose, why?" He said, "She was agitated and I gave her too much." Against his wishes I had Dr. Morrison in the room. I asked him if Lorraine would die without the PEG tube and he said "Yes." I then told Dr. Morrison to put the PEG into Lorraine's stomach. On Friday October 23, 2009 he placed the PEG into Lorraine's stomach. At this point I was forced to find a skilled nursing facility. I asked a social worker to recommend one that had a good rehabilitation program because I wanted to try to get her strong and bring her home. She recommended The Nursing Home of the Angel. I went down on Monday, October 26, 2009 and made arrangements for her late that afternoon. Dr. Camel made us wait over three hours before discharging us and then sent his partner with a faxed discharge.

At The Nursing Home of the Angel, she was under the care of a fine doctor, a compassionate man who tried his best to keep her alive. The nursing was sensational and the rehab unbelievable. Unfortunately she had another stroke one week after she was there and got pneumonia in the last two weeks. On December 31, 2009, she passed away from Aspiration Pneumonia from the Zyprexa given to her by Dr. Camel. Again the FDA said elderly people with dementia and psychosis die from it. Dr. Camel was not phased by the FDA Black Box warning. He gave it to her anyway. He is responsible for her death because he gave her the Zyprexa; and an overdose for good measure.

This whole chapter is documented in her medical records and in the complaint form I made against him.

My wife's death was not necessary. A wonderful woman was killed by a rogue doctor and I hope this story gets published and the powers of doctors get laid to rest forever. He has to be accountable and those responsible for helping him avoid prosecution will pay the price.

If I may, I would like to return to the nursing home of the angel. I was looking for a Good rehab nursing home and as I said on the previous page I got the best. There was a therapist on the staff called Scott. They named him "Peter Pan" because he worked miracles with his patients and he worked on my wife Monday – Friday from 1pm to 3pm. He not only worked her arms, neck & legs but he stood her up. He would take a sheet, twirl it till it looked like a thin python and wrapped it around her waist and his own waist. One of the other members of the unit put a pillow between both of them and Peter Pan would yell to Lorraine to "stand up" and he would pull at the sheet and she stood up and never moved or faltered. Every staff member clapped as I did. I also yelled "great job hon" and told everyone "that's my darling." My goal for Lorraine was to improve her condition sufficiently to permit her enjoy optimum quality of life and if possible, to return home with visiting nurses care. Lorraine worked diligently in her rehab and with the dedicated care of the therapists and clinical support of the specialists. That wasn't going to be because in addition to the stroke she had at Crater Hospital from the Zeprexa she got another one at the Nursing Home of the Angel. She died December 31, 2009 of Aspiration Pneumonia.

All the while watching Lorraine do her rehab I had the feeling I should do something for the nursing home so they will never forget my wonderful wife. I asked the administrator if he had any projects outside on the patio that I could take care of. He said yes, a planned fountain for the patio. I immediately said "that's for me." I got together with the maintenance men and I funded the entire operation. There was a hill outside with a broken down fence and stumps and debris all over the hill. They got construction going, carried rocks in the hot sun, and cleaned it up. The Admissions Director took me to buy an angel, part of the hill was removed and we placed her on a perch near flowing water that ended into a pond. Absolutely beautiful. The whole garden is a tribute to my dear wife and for the wonderful members of the staff, the residents, and the visiting family members to enjoy. It's truly a serenity garden in memory of my dear wife. The dedication was a year later and the beautiful angel was officially named by me as The Angel Lorraine.

There is a picture of my wife and me on the wall at the entrance to the patio to show the people entering "our garden" the inspiration for it and there is also a plaque in the garden as tribute to my wife acknowledging who she was and why the garden was built. Now she will always be remembered for her courage and determination to live for us. She is in my thoughts and prayers every day and in my heart always. My love for her is undying and everything I do is in honor of her. The Nursing Home of the Angel is my home away from home. I go there every opportunity I get. I am there weekends and whenever I can during the week. I am proud to say that I am an official volunteer at the home. During the summer months we feed the residents outside on the patio where they are in plain view of the angel I also continue to make contributions to a fund started by me for anything they need. I love the staff and the residents alike. I will never forget how well my wife was treated at the home and I am sure the families of the residents feel the same as I do. My wife was my whole life when she was alive and revere her and do everything with her name as the person helping someone or providing the home with something. This is my way to memorialize her. Everyone knows who I am, who she was, and what the angel represents.

LORRAINE'S LEGACY

Lorraine will be remembered always. I'm making sure of that with the book and word of mouth and she has done well for herself too. In some respects she has changed people's lives and mostly her own. She was a physically abused girl by a drunken father who saw fit to come home from work and want and did beat his wife, daughter and son. Lorraine changed that by being a fighter for her mother and brother. She took on the task of making her father to change his ways and to respect his family. As afraid as she was, she saw to it that he stopped drinking and be a good member of his home and to the community. When I met and fell in love with her I swore at that moment she would never have a bad day in her life again. I kept my promise and we had a beautiful life and loved each other dearly. Oh, yes, her father stopped drinking and was a pretty good guy. She forgot the past and the bad times and concentrated on the good life.

Every life Lorraine touched changed the life. That young 12 year old girl in Richmond, VA in the candy store we saw in the store on another trip. She was now a sales girl in that very store. If Lorraine didn't do what she had done some years sooner, what and where would the girl be doing now.

This is how Lorraine impacted people's lives she met. She is also known in a negative way. Not what she did, but what was done to her. We know from the rest of the book she was killed by Dr. Camel at Crater Memorial Hospital those who know her and me are quite aware of the medication Zyprexa was given to her and against the orders of the FDA to not give elderly people with Dementia and Psychosis because they die. My wife had Dementia with Psychosis and she died. All this done behind my back. All those who knew us are wary of the medication and the doctors name and the hospital. So my wife is unknowingly saving lives just because they know what happened to her and those who don't know her and read the book will know who she is.

When I had to put her in a nursing home after the doctor's work left her unable to walk, talk, eat, swallow or see and two strokes she died on December 31, 2009 from Aspiration Pneumonia. In her honor and her biggest legacy would be the garden I had built with a hill, an angel that I named the Angel Lorraine perched on a cut piece of the hill with water running down along side and around her in a pond and some gorgeous flowers and some plants planted in the beautiful garden. The impact: everyone, the staff, the residents all love the garden and the angel. People from the community come to see it and marvel at it in the summer months residents are fed at various times out on the patio where the garden is located. Also at various times and occasions the staff enjoy the grilled food with the activities director. I myself as a volunteer am proud to help serve the food. Outside the patio on the wall as you open the door to go out is a picture of my wife and myself, so you know the name when you go out and the plaque in the garden itself everyone knows the garden and especially the angel. When they look at the angel they are at peace and also see a woman of courage who tried her hardest to live, but the doctor's medication killed her anyway, he killed a beautiful woman inside and out.

Lorraine is leaving the footprint of a person that has gained the respect of all who knew her or met her or was the recipient of a smile from her with her beautiful white teeth is a lucky person because whether they know it or not are contributing to Lorraine's Legacy and will be a part of history knowing an individual who touched their life.

Lorraine was honest, sincere, loving, full of life, had a good heart and soul and was a good person who loved her God and just about everyone in his kingdom. They didn't come any better then my wife. Everyone touched by her is a better person for it. I never heard anyone speak ill of her and that's because how do you speak ill of a true angel of God. When I bought her for the hill she was ordered and the mold was made. She was not but the property of a monument seller. Her name was Gabrielle and I changed it to the Angel Lorraine in reference to her at the dedication of the garden on our anniversary August 29, 2010. My angel, and everybody who needs her!

RECOLLECTIONS OF LORRAINE

1. ICE SKATING AT ROCKEFELLER CENTER

I mentioned this in the chapter on "How we met and our life since Nov. 25, 1972." We had lunch at the Piccadilly Hotel and since it was Christmas time (her favorite time of year) we decided to go ice skating at Rockefeller Center. Lorraine has been ice skating before but I have not. We had so much fun ice skating. We fell over each other as well as other people skating. There was a nice variety of skaters. Some couldn't skate like me, others were able to skate like Lorraine, and then there were the show-offs. Then the fall Lorraine has been waiting for happened. It was perfect. We had just tangled with another couple and as the four of us fell Lorraine shouted "See my beau and I have fallen for each other and we are very much in love And we are getting married, right hon?" I quickly said "YES! YES! YES!" The other couple said "Congratulations. Let's drink to that" So the four of us left the ice and went to a nearby table and toasted to us. That was my baby, one and a half years later we were married. To this day just thinking about it brings a smile to my face, then the tears, and finally laughter.

2. EATING WATERMELON

Lorraine had a love of watermelon. In the summer there would always be 2 bowls of fresh cut watermelon. Whenever I would come home from shopping I would always leave the watermelon in the car parked in the garage. She would come running into the kitchen looking for her watermelon and I would playful slap my forehead as if to say I forgot. She knew better having done this many times before. She would run to the door to the garage and pointed at the car and would laugh. She was too smart for my tricks even though she was suffering with Dementia. So I would cut up the watermelon and chill it in the refrigerator and after supper call Lorraine out to the kitchen. We would stand by the sink and I would feed her piece by piece. She enjoyed it so much, every few pieces she would point to my mouth as if to say "Now you Hon." She was absolutely wonderful. She wanted to share everything with me: Her life, her love and even her watermelon.

3. WANTING TO HELP AFTER MY SURGERY

In the late summer of 2009 I had surgery to close a hole in the macula of my right eye. After the surgery while recovering at home I was ordered to lay on my stomach face down and only get up to go to the bathroom or to eat. I only did this for four days and after a checkup with the doctor he determined the surgery was not working. He said it has closed partially so it would not get any worse. The reason for this story is to describe my wife's love. After being diagnosed with dementia in 2005 and as sick as she was she sensed I needed help. She came in my room one day and asked "Do you need any help hon?" I replied "No thank you baby, I'm okay. I am going to get up soon and make us dinner."

I will always remember that day when my beautiful wife came to help the man she loved. I loved her so much and to this day I still do. The memory of that day will live forever. We had one heart, one soul.

4. THE DAY SHE DIED

It was Thursday, December 31, 2009, when Lorraine's oxygen level dropped to 40 and a STAT was called. The doctors at Little Forks Hospital requested that I leave the room while they worked on my wife. As she was being taken to ICU with an oxygen tube in her mouth I grabbed her hand and held the tight while she was being taken through the halls. When we reached the room they asked me to go wait in the waiting room. I could not stand to be apart from her. I took a seat closest to her room and sat nervously. A few minutes later a nurse came out and had me sign a request form for them to insert a suction tube in her chest. Feeling a little relief I signed figuring they would be able to suction the fluid out of her. Instead after about a half hour a doctor came out to inform me the procedure was hopeless. The mucus in her chest had already began to emulsify and wouldn't fit in the tube. Naturally I cried and begged for him to try again. He obliged but the next time he returned to me was to inform me she had passed. Cause of death was Aspiration Pneumonia.

After they cleaned her up I went in to say goodbye and was amazed at what I saw. The pull of her lips caused by her 2 previous strokes were gone. Her beautiful blue eyes were open and back to normal. Her lips were full and her cheeks were rosy. It was the most beautiful I have ever seen her. I kissed my wife repeatedly and pleaded for her to come back to me. After about 45 minutes the nurse came in and asked me to leave, I wanted to stay with her forever. The story is far from over. In the weeks following my wife's passing I began to seek psychiatric help for my grief. The first thing I asked her was "What happened to my wife in that hospital room?". She told me that God had given me a gift. God was telling me that he was taking care of her now. And that she will be in his arms as one of his angels. I believe whole heartedly what she told me. I still recall the way she looked and I am thankful to the Lord for taking care of one of his most beautiful angels.

THANK GOD FOR GOD

The following is the most startling story of the book and was and always will remain forever in my heart. It is from the chapter "Recollections of Lorraine: The day she died" and it bears repeating. For God came into my life after my wife was gone.

Two big differences between the two are: The first version is medical and factual and the second version is emotional and spiritual.

This is the second time I have written about our Lord God. Why? Because my darling wife Lorraine is, as of December 31, 2009, one of God's angels. I was in the room at Little Forks hospital in Little Forks,

PA. When the miracle of all miracles took place, she was ready to take her place in Heaven, Lorraine was a beautiful woman but now had become the most beautiful woman I had ever seen in my life... she defied all imagination. Her lips were rid of the pull to the side of her face because of the two strokes she had; one at Crater Memorial Hospital and the other at The Nursing Home of the Angel and now her lips were normal and full; her cheeks were rosy as could be and her gorgeous blue eyes were open and sparkling as never before; her beautiful short cut white colored hair was combed to perfection for her trip to the Kingdom of Heaven. My love was about to become an angel. The Lord honored me by my being allowed to see her all prepared. Then there was something else. I looked into her beautiful eyes and cried for her to come back to me. I kissed her face and her eyes endlessly. The tears did not stop and they were all over her face and eyes. It was like she was crying too and our tears were mixing together and our hearts and our souls will forever be as it has been when we saw each other for the first time on November 25, 1972 and fell deeply in love and became one heart and one soul. The pain in my aching heart was too much to bear. If she couldn't come back to me, I wanted to go with her. All I ever wanted in this world or any other world was to be with my darling mate Lorraine. I will love her and miss her till the day that I die. When I left that room I knew what my mission was from that point on: I had to bring the killer of my wife to justice. Not to use violence for the Lord said "Vengeance is mine". On December 31, 2013 it will be four years since she died at 10:55am on that date in 2009. The doctor who is the culprit has escaped prosecution and culpability for his crime against my wife with much help but he won't escape God's punishment. I had my doubts but I prayed to God for patience and he answered my prayers with no more doubts or fears for me and I know in the Lord's time there will be justice for my wife and the helpers who will cry for mercy. Let's see how formidable they are against the Lord, and not against a helpless elderly sick person fed pills to deliberately kill her.

LIFE AFTER LORRAINE

I gave you some anecdotes about my darling Lorraine. She was beautiful, kind, funny, generous, a good wife, loyal, a fantastic dancer, and a good cook of southern food. There is more to say, but I want to talk about me without her. I have a medal that says: "When I miss you the most I look deep into my heart and find you there." That's where she is and always was there from the moment I looked into the most gorgeous blue eyes I had ever seen. I close mine now and see them before me. I miss her terribly. When you have a life as wonderful as we did you become a lone wolf and can't & won't accept the fact that she's gone. I'm not a stupid man. My mind knows I'll never see her again till the lord unites us for eternity. It's been 3 years and 4 months and it never gets easier. I wrote in another chapter that I moved to a gated community and gave away everything in it and then sold it. Lorraine designed it and we had it built and now somebody else owns it and if they have half the happiness we had in it then they will be very lucky. I belong to the American Association of Retired Persons and they had this to say about ISOLATION: As people age, isolation is a major cause of decline in <u>physical Mental </u>and <u>emotional </u>well-being. This is a very true fact. I am completely alone and talk every day to whoever I can. The silence is deafening. When you're with your mate for nearly 38 years and then in two and a half months she's gone at the hands of the doctor and his partner in crime The Physician's Assistant Certified Psychiatry, the shock is immediate. Suddenly you're alone and crying for her all the time and just can't believe what is happening to you. I was grieving so bad I went into therapy and go 2 times a week. From January 2010 I knew what I had to do and that was to get justice for my wife. I tried lawyers but they wanted nothing to do with this area. I was then going to try for justice with the medical board but was closed down twice. The system failed my wife and me too. The only place that never hurt me is The Nursing Home of the Angel where my wife dear wife had to go and she died at Little Forks Hospital December 31, 2009 from Aspiration Pneumonia. My wife's story has been well documented in this book. I want all people to know what happened to her and how I was treated trying to get justice for my deceased wife. I try my best to be positive but when I think about her and that's all the time, I see her back with me. I know I should be remembering what a beautiful life we had and the love we had for each other. One day soon my memories of her will be good and not cry. There are some times when I look at the 8 x 10 photos of her and laugh when I remember the "good days"

I'm glad I have the Nursing Home of the Angel to go to and visit my staff friends and sit outside at the garden and talk to the angel and anyone else who is there. I am an official volunteer there and we will be feeding the residents outside and the staff on certain special days.

There will come a day after the book is published when the book is well read that my wife and I will at last get justice and hopefully there will be less men or women left alone because a doctor just did anything he wanted with his patient and finally be accountable for their actions.

With the help of my therapist I will heal but I'll never stop loving my dear, beautiful wife. This book clearly shows what happened to my wife at Crater Memorial Hospital and will clearly show the doctors guilt. I have an air-tight case against him and the medical board let him escape from being charged and prosecuted. I've been searching for my day in court. I never seeked monetary gain, only justice! This has been my life after my wife was torn from me, not taken. There is a hole in my heart that cannot be repaired. Lorraine and I were one person. We were always together. I never wanted to be anywhere except with her, and she felt the same. We had one heart and one soul. That's why I don't care about anything unless it is about my wife or concerning the book. I don't go anywhere except to the doctors or to the Nursing Home of the Angel. I feel safe there and I love the staff and the residents alike.

The home has been my salvation. The title of this chapter is Life after Lorraine. There is no life for me after Lorraine. I go where I have to and then to the house where there is nobody but me. From the moment she died I've had one mission and anybody who knows me: says justice for Lorraine and since I was sold out at the state level, the mission is the book. If I'm to complete the mission I have to start taking care of myself or I should say better care of myself. I need to be strong for the finish. I can't be falling apart like I do. The loneliness brings the devil and I'm going to work harder to keep him at bay. I have God on my side and my angel wife too. I pray for help from both of them to keep me healthy. I'm the only one I have control over so I will make a great effort from now on. The book is the most important thing I have ever done in my life and I will be there first at the finish line.

ENDING

If I had an issue with somebody I, like my wife, Lorraine, would always say, "so what did he or she do to me, KILL ME?" With that expression it was all over. If she said to me now,: "So what did they do, KILL ME?" I would have to say, "Yes Hon, they did!"

Pages from Lorraine's Medical Records at Crater Memorial Hospital

Lorraine was my dear and beloved wife whose only crime was getting dementia with psychosis. She didn't die from dementia but instead from Aspiration Pneumonia at the hands of a doctor who put her down with a drug called Zyprexa, which the FDA said was not approved for her condition. Behind my back, he gave it to her anyway and she died from one of the two prominent causes of death to the elderly with dementia with psychosis: 1) Cardiovascular and 2) Aspiration Pneumonia. He never consulted with me about the drug or putting her DNR, which he put her on her first day in the hospital. He played God and killed my wife.

The pages are from her medical records I obtained at Crater Memorial Hospital with a Power of Attorney when she was at the Nursing home of the Angel before she died. Each page will be noted with all his wrong-doings that finally cost her her life, just two and a half months from the time she walked into the hospital under her own power until her death at his hands. The pages are noted with all his lies.

All comments on the following pages that are circled are solely the authors.

They are not the thoughts or opinion of any of the doctors, nurses or medical staff.

PHYSICIAN'S ORDERS

NOTE:
AUTHORIZATION IS HEREBY GIVEN TO
DISPENSE THIS GENERIC OR CHEMICAL
EQUIVALENT UNLESS SPECIFICALLY
CIRCLED BY THE PHYSICIAN.

Instructions: 1. Imprint patient's name before placing chart.
2. Sent to Pharmacy

DATE & TIME	NURSE'S INITIALS & TIME	PHYSICIAN'S ORDERS AND SIGNATURES - USE BALL POINT PEN
10/7/09 10:10		#1 _Admit to General Medical floor_
		#2 _Dr ABN wet us, Dennison & Psychara_
		#3 _Diet regular_
		#4 _Activity as tolerated bed with Supervision_
		#5 _Because of Dennison & Psychara keep Closely Supervised_
		#6 _Dx_
		CBC, BMP, B12, Folate, lipn profile, TSH
		#7 _T4_
		IM IM q4° PRN Agitation.
		Tylenol 650m PO Q4° PRN Pain
		#8 _Consult Psychiatry : Dennison & Psychara_
		#9 _Consult DNR : Dennison & Psychara_
		#10 _Consult Care Management SNF_

(HE WANTED HER DEAD)

SCANNED
Name:
Circle one: HUD _GN LPN RN_
Date & Time: 10/10/09 11:10

VERBAL ORDER
TO THE NURSE
THE FIRST DAY WITH
NO DISCUSSION WITH
ME

FIRST DAY	10/7/09 1:55	DNR W/this & information	←

K1 10/7/09 1:55

DRUG ALLERGIES
NKA

noted 10/7/09

Patient Identification

30-84-56
075 Y F

10/07/2009
MEDICARE
BLUE CROSS

THE
DR. HAS
TO SIGN
BUT ME
NEVER CONSULTS WITH

PO-9 (IPO) MRC-723, FORMS 7/04 REVIEWED 4/09

PROGRESS NOTES

DATE	TIME	
		↓ VERBAL ORDER DNR TO NURSE
10-7-09	1155	pt is a dnr aspir pr. BY ___
10/8/09	12¹¹	Nutrition ✶ AND THE NURSE SIGNED ✶
		Plan) Recommend Ensure Plus BID - chocolate. — pt is unable to take our healthshakes & milk bas ___ req × ___
8 OCT 09	1235	Input free Versus ~~Busseratt~~ is generall DLH so north & hecheppy in general B12 is low NML.
10/8/09	1700	Psych
		D - Oriented to name only. Some ↑ agitation this afternoon where pt required IM Zyprexa 5mg. Pt seen earlier today ~ 11am and appeared much calmer than yesterday. Speech remains garbled. ⊕ internal preoccupation: Noted to respond to stimuli. Started back on Excelon patches per Excelancerme) Neuro. A/P - Advanced Dementia - cont Zyprexa 5mg HS ē PRN Zyprexa 5mg IMQ

DRUG ALLERGIES Placement most likely needed P NC

(HER NERVE)

NS-14 MRC-29
FORMS 6/00, REVIEWED 3/09

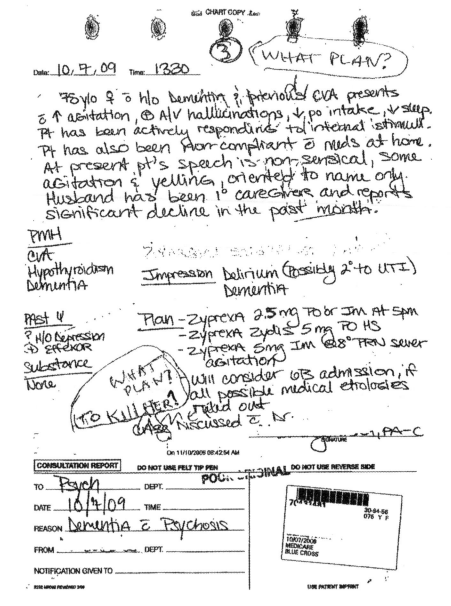

③ (WHAT PLAN?)

Date: 10, 7, 09   Time: 1330

75 y/o ♀ ō h/o Dementia ? previous CVA presents
ō ↑ agitation, ⊕ A/V hallucinations, ↓ po intake, ↓ sleep.
Pt has been actively responding to internal stimuli.
Pt has also been poor compliant ō meds at home.
At present, pt's speech is non-sensical, some
agitation & yelling, oriented to name only.
Husband has been 1° caregiver and reports
significant decline in the past month.

PMH
CVA
Hypothyroidism
Dementia

Impression Delirium (possibly 2° to UTI)
            Dementia

PAST ₡
? H/o Depression
⊕ Effexor
Substance
None

Plan - Zyprexa 2.5 mg PO or IM At 5pm
     - Zyprexa Zydis 5 mg PO HS
     - Zyprexa 5mg IM @8° PRN sever
       agitation

(WHAT PLAN? TO KILL HER?) Will consider GB admission, if
all possible medical etiologies
ruled out
Case discussed ō N.

_____ PA-C
SIGNATURE

On 11/10/2009 08:42:54 AM

CONSULTATION REPORT   DO NOT USE FELT TIP PEN   DO NOT USE REVERSE SIDE

TO Psych _____ DEPT. _____

DATE 10/7/09 ____ TIME _____

REASON Dementia ō Psychosis

FROM _____ DEPT. _____

NOTIFICATION GIVEN TO _____

3232 MR042 REVISED 3/99

70   30-94-56
            078 Y F
10/07/2008
MEDICARE
BLUE CROSS

USE PATIENT IMPRINT

- 138 -

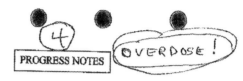

（4）

PROGRESS NOTES OVERDOSE!

DATE	TIME	
13 OCT 09	1545	Still a bit overly sedated & perhaps it is a fn of not only the one 10mg dose but a cumulative dose since hospitalization. Her elevation, cognition & psyche on indeed quite normal & now a therapeutic objective & I appreciate the follow-up. _(signature)_
		(circled) ADMITS HERE HE GAVE HER THE 10 MG. OVERDOSE & ALSO GAVE HER ZYPREXA 15.0 FIRST DAY SHE WAS IN THE HOSPITAL " SINCE HOSPITALIZATION !!

DRUG ALLERGIES

Patient Identification

30-94-56
07B Y F
10/07/2009
MEDICARE
BLUE CROSS

PHYSICIAN'S ORDERS

⑤

STAT

NOTE:
AUTHORIZATION IS HEREBY GIVEN TO
DISPENSE THE GENERIC OR CHEMICAL
EQUIVALENT UNLESS SPECIFICALLY
CIRCLED BY THE PHYSICIAN.

Instructions: 1. Imprint patient's name before placing chart.
2. Scan to Pharmacy

(circled handwritten note, top): 10 MG OVERDOSE IN THE EVENING AFTER ALREADY GIVING HER 5 IN THE DAYTIME

DATE & TIME	NURSE'S INITIALS & TIME	PHYSICIAN'S ORDERS AND SIGNATURES - USE BALL POINT PEN
10/09/09 1415	10/09	*(signature)* 10/10/09 16:00
11/08/09 1210		Continue 1:1 attendance → DOUBLE OVERDOSE Ambulate as able with assistance *(illeg.)* 10 mg PO N.S

SCANNED
Name
Circle one ... LPN RN
Date & Time 10/10/09 1210

10/11/09

8° ✓ 10/12/09 0730

DRUG ALLERGIES

(circled handwritten note, bottom): HE OVERDOSED HER WHEN I TOLD HIM I WAS TAKING HER HOME — WITH HE OVERDOSED HER NO MEDS ASSISTANCE AND SIGN THE HIM OUT AT THE TIME

Patient Identification

70_____ 30-94-66
075 Y F

10/07/2009
MEDICARE
BLUE CROSS

PO-9 (IPO) MRC-723, FORMS 7/04 REVIEWED 4/09

- 140 -

(6)

PUT A PEG IN HER STOMACH SO SHE CAN LIVE

PROGRESS NOTES

HE WANTS ME TO PUT HER DOWN AFTER HE HIMSELF DOES THIS TO HER

DATE	TIME	
22/10/09	0450	Obtunded,
		124/62 T99.2.
		No JVD, Diffuse rhonchi & upper airway noises.
		heart reg w/ edema.
		Ext @ [illegible]
		Hx: CVA
		Parkinson's & Resp failure
		Dementia
		Plan: She, her husband wishes all to be done.
		I have explained that dementia is a terminal
		illness & place that in the setting of
		CVA & Parkinson the outcome is not good
		& palliative treatment would be humane.
		But not resolving here he desires full
		Code Status & a PEG tube

"PUT HER DOWN" HE SAYS MORE, MORE HUMANE

I TOLD HIM YOU DID THIS!

Patient Identification

DRUG ALLERGIES *

DIMENTIA DIDN'T DO THIS TO HER HIZ ZYPREXA DID AND NOW HE WANTS TO PUT HER DOWN. THAT KILLER

70431481

30-84-56
075 Y F

10/07/2009
MEDICARE
BLUE CROSS

NS-14 MRC-29
FORMS 6/00, REVIEWED 3/09

LIE — NO DISCUSSIONS WITH DR. ON DNR OR ANYTHING

DATE	TIME	
15 oct 09	1815	On 13 oct I was called @ 2300 from RN for fever. I cultured & did a CXR. The x-ray demonstrated pneumonia. I reviewed how I tx'ed it w/ Mr Gardner. Placed her on ceftriaxone & floxal. She & her husband has felt grateful received the DNR status. Unfortunately, I was not here to guide [illegible] has advanced Dementia. [illegible] Obtunded. [illegible] ccc, chest pc, [illegible] no edema. Lab WBC 19,000
		Plan Palm Care. I Discussed c husband about DNR — & she may come around to a Comfortable decision.

LIE
HE NEVER HAD ANY DISCUSSION WITH ME

DRUG ALLERGIES

7043 401   30-94-66
                075 Y F
10/07/2009
MEDICARE
BLUE CROSS

NS-14 MRC-29
FORMS 6/00, REVIEW 3/09

Patient Identification

PROGRESS NOTES

DATE	TIME	
	10/10/05	"Mel) A) very lethargic
	2:00PM	O/F
		— 160/100 P8?
		lung - clear
		CUE S̄
		A AMS → lethargy
		Dementia
		Pla ↓ Zyprexa ← cause
10/12/09	1:00	Psych
		A — Sedated entire day. Had ↑ dose of
		Zyprexa last night (10mg). Pt's husband
		insisting that he takes her home. He remains
		in denial about the severity of wife's dementia.
		Excepting of social service consult but only if
		is the one to contact them.
		A/P Advanced Dementia— Hold Zyprexa tonight

DRUG ALLERGIES NC ☐ script of zyprexa EMG A/P Dean

NS-14 MRC-29
FORMS 6/00, REVIEWED 3/09

70 31491   30-94-56   075 Y F
10/07/2009
MEDICARE
BLUE CROSS

(CRUSHED PILLS IN THE CHOCOLATE PUDDING)

DATE 10/11/09
TIME 0745

(9)

At one 1:1 observation. Talking constantly and listening to voices.
Sitting up in chair - talking to self. Assist c bbpd & bath.

(1000) Lg. amt of very lg amt loose brown stool. Un cooperative
during diaper ∆, pericare c 3 assist.

(1100) Agitation increased + did not sleep last night. (Olanzapine)
5 mg orally disintegrating tab. Given c pudding.

(1200) Pt in bed c much calmer. Able to rest.

(1600) Still resting in bed. Eval pt & grow home
again back to chair @ 1800.

Continue as above. O vs changes.

1930 Alert and oriented x 3 Breathing easy. defence
denies pain. lying in bed 1:1 obs continuation
continues. 2200 awake lying in bed. took medication
and asleep. 0200 no change in status. 0400 asleep.
0600 asleep. O poss elmst O

(Crushed pills in the pudding)
(some people !!)

TO BE COMPLETED DAILY.

SENSORY PERCEPTION	MOISTURE	ACTIVITY	MOBILITY	NUTRITION	FRICTION SHEAR	
COMP. LIMITED 4	CONSTANT 4	BED FAST 4	COMP. IMMOBILE 4	VERY POOR 4		TOTAL SCORE
VERY LIMITED 3	VERY 3	CHAIR FAST 3	VERY LIMITED 3	PROB. INADEQ. 3	PROBLEM 3	
SLIGHTLY LIMITED 2	OCCAS 2	WALKS OCCAS 2	SLIGHTLY LIMITED 2	ADEQUATE 2	POTENTIAL 2	
NO IMPAIR. 1	RARELY 1	WALKS FREQ. 1	NO LIMITED 1	EXCELLENT 1	NO PROB. 1	
1	2	2	2	3	2	12

SKIN PROTOCOL INITIATED:
☐ ↓ 12 LOW RISK   ☑ 12-14 MOD. RISK   ☐ 15 HIGH RISK

Time _____

```
70431481          30-94-56
                  075 Y F
```

10/07/2009
MEDICARE
BLUE CROSS

PATIENT STAMP

S.A.F.E. Tool (circle scores)	
Risk Factor	Score
History of Falls	3
Age over 65	(1)
Confused / Disoriented	(1)(1)
Impaired Judgment / Memory	1
Sensory Deficit (hearing, vision)	1
Unable to Ambulate Independently	(1)(1)
Uncooperative / Anxious / Agitated	1
Incontinent / Diarrhea	(1)
Frequency / Urgency	1
Postural Hypotension w/dizziness	1
Medications affecting BP or LOC	›1
Polypharmacy (more than 4 meds)	1
Perfusion / Oxygenation affected by	1
Cardiovascular / Respiratory Disease	
Attached Equipment (IV pole, oxygen tubing, appliances, etc.)	1

Total Score _____

High Risk Safety Protocol for total score of 5 or greater.

Time 0745   Signature _____ RN

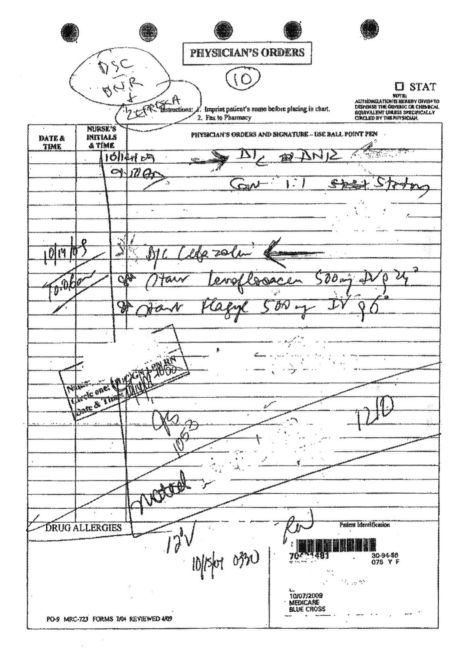

PHYSICIAN'S ORDERS

(10)

☐ STAT

Instructions: 1. Imprint patient's name before placing in chart.
2. Fax to Pharmacy

DATE & TIME	NURSE'S INITIALS & TIME	PHYSICIAN'S ORDERS AND SIGNATURE – USE BALL POINT PEN
	10/14/09	D/C ANI2
		Con 1:1 Start Sitting
10/14/08		D/C Cefazolin
10:06		Start Levofloxacin 500mg IV q24°
		Start Flagyl 500mg IV q8°

DRUG ALLERGIES

Patient Identification

(11)

NOTES:

10/14/09 1400

Chart Reviewed-

1. Husband [illegible] status- "wants everything done"

2. Request for HHA agency - husband [illegible] preference

follow for DME needs @ DC-

possible H.B, BSC, O2, bed alarm

3. Clinical reviewed- [illegible] progress notes

indicate pneumonia - on IVAbx, O2,

medical workup ongoing

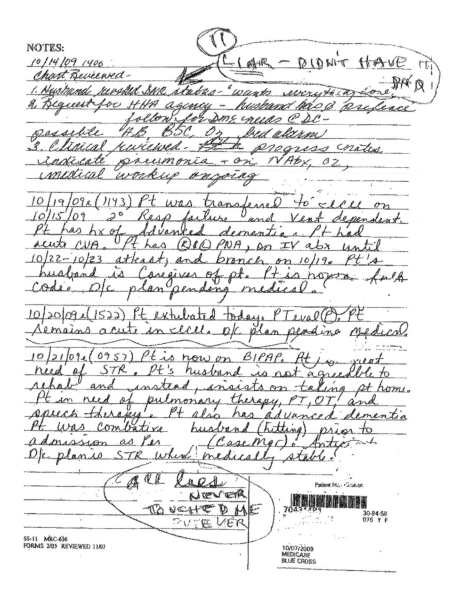

LIAR - DIDN'T HAVE IT! PNA!

10/19/09e (1143) Pt was transferred to CCU on 10/15/09 2° Resp failure and Vent dependent. Pt has hx of Advanced dementia. Pt had acute CVA. Pt has (R)&(L) PNA, on IV abx until 10/22-10/23 atleast, and branch on 10/19. Pt's husband is Caregiver of pt. Pt is [illegible] full Code. D/c plan pending medical.

10/20/09e (1522) Pt extubated today. PT eval (P). Pt remains acute in CCU. D/c plan pending medical.

10/21/09e (0957) Pt is now on BIPAP. Pt in great need of STR. Pt's husband is not agreeable to rehab and instead, insists on taking pt home. Pt in need of pulmonary therapy, PT, OT, and speech therapy. Pt also has advanced dementia. Pt was combative husband (hitting) prior to admission as Per (Case Mgr). Antic[illegible] D/c plan is STR when medically stable.

ALL LIES NEVER TOUCHED ME EVER EVER

Patient [illegible]

704[illegible] 30-94-58 076 Y F

10/07/2009
MEDICARE
BLUE CROSS

SS-11 MRC-636
FORMS 2/03 REVIEWED 11/07

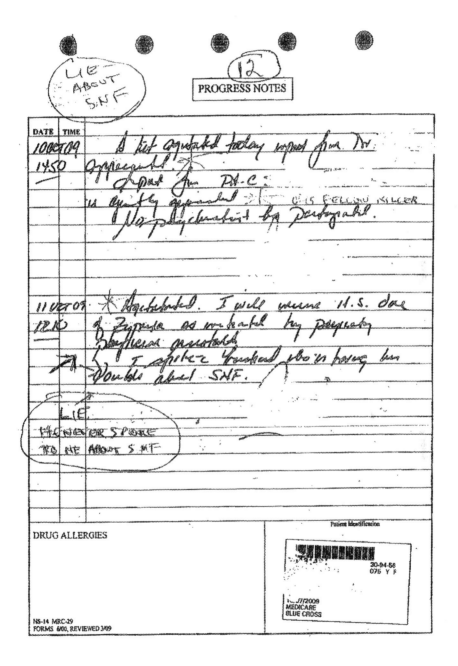

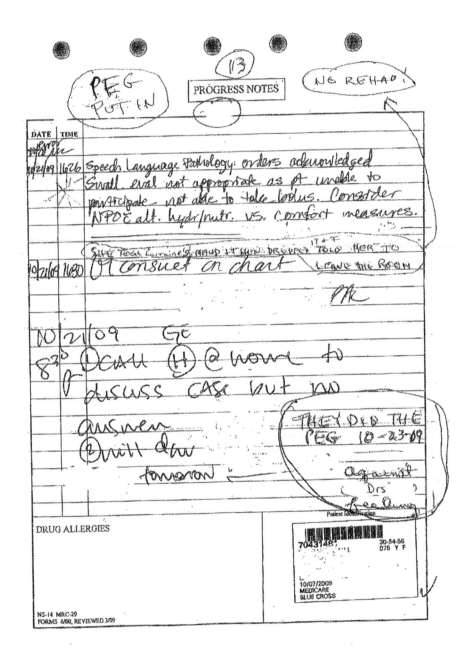

(PEG PUT IN)

PROGRESS NOTES (13)

(NO REHAB!)

DATE	TIME	
10/2/09	1626	Speech Language Pathology: orders acknowledged. Swall eval not appropriate as pt unable to participate, not able to take bolus. Consider NPO c̄ alt. hydr/nutr. vs. comfort measures.
		Spike Team Corrine's group - IT had dropped IT + F TOLD HER TO
10/21/09	1650	OT consult on chart LEAVE THE ROOM
		PK

10/2/09   GE
8³⁰ ① call ⓗ @ home to
      discuss case but no
      answer
      ② will draw
         tomorrow

THEY DID THE
PEG 10-23-09

Against
(Drs)
Lee Ann

Patient Identification

DRUG ALLERGIES

7043148   30-54-56
            075 Y F

10/07/2009
MEDICARE
BLUE CROSS

NS-14 MRC-29
FORMS 6/00, REVIEWED 3/09

- 148 -

DATE 10/07/09 (WHAT NEW ORDERS?) **NURSES NOTES** (14) (162)
TIME 1100

Patient arrived on the unit alert but [illegible] and [illegible] able to get patient to walk from doorway to her bed with assist of two. Patient is not easily directed. [illegible] is present [illegible]. Patient is unable to use call light. Bed alarm is in place, clothes clip alarm also applied, both alarms are functional. 1:1 [illegible] also obtained, [illegible] in room [illegible]. Unable to obtain [illegible] access due to patient's [illegible] to be attempted once patient is settled. [illegible] Patient continues to be agitated [illegible] administered per orders. Care ongoing. 1400 Patient was seen by PA Psych, new orders noted. 1630 Patient sitting [illegible] in chair at bedside, ate 98% of dinner. 1:1 continues. Occasional verbal outburst heard. [illegible] also at bedside. 1830 Patient remains confused, sitting up in chair at bedside, much calmer as per admission time. Care is ongoing. [illegible] 10/7/09 1900-0730 - [illegible] Pt [illegible] confused [illegible] does not answer questions appropriately or follow instructions. Pt continues to have 1:1 [illegible] for safety. [illegible] 20% [illegible] agitated & [illegible].

*TO BE COMPLETED DAILY.

SENSORY PERCEPTION	MOISTURE	ACTIVITY	MOBILITY	NUTRITION	FRICTION SHEAR	TOTAL SCORE
COMP. LIMITED 4	CONSTANT 4	BED FAST 4	COMP. IMMOBILE 4	VERY POOR 4		
VERY LIMITED 3	VERY 3	CHAIR FAST 3	VERY LIMITED 3	PROB INADEQ. 3	PROBLEM 3	
SLIGHTLY LIMITED 2	OCCAS 2	WALKS OCCAS 2	SLIGHTLY LIMITED 2	ADEQUATE 2	POTENTIAL 2	
NO IMPAIR. 1	RARELY 1	WALKS FREQ. 1	NO LIMITED 1	EXCELLENT 1	NO PROB. 1	
1	1	2	2	2	1	9

SIGN PROTOCOL INITIATED:
☒ 12 LOW RISK ☐ 12-14 MOD. RISK ☐ 15 HIGH RISK

Time 1100 Signature [illegible]

70411491 30-94-56 075 Y F

10/07/2009
MEDICARE
BLUE CROSS
PATIENT STAMP

*TO BE COMPLETED DAILY.

FALL RISK ASSESSMENT

S.A.F.E. Tool (circle scores)	
Risk Factor	Score
History of Falls	3
Age over 65	(1)
Confused / Disoriented	(1)
Impaired judgment / Memory	(1)
Sensory Deficit (hearing, vision)	1
Unable to Ambulate Independently	(1)
Uncooperative / Anxious / Agitated	1
Incontinent / Diarrhea	(1)
Frequency / Urgency	1
Postural Hypotension w/dizziness	1
Medications affecting BP or LOC	1
Polypharmacy (more than 4 meds)	1
Perfusion / Oxygenation affected by Cardiovascular / Respiratory Disease	1
Attached Equipment (IV pole, oxygen tubing, appliances, etc.)	1
Total Score	5
High Risk Safety Protocol for total score of 5 or greater.	

Time 1100 Signature [illegible]

15

DSC / DNR

PROGRESS NOTES

DATE	TIME	
10/14/09		Deval/MD
		A/ she very lethargic
		Temp 101
		lung Roll at Base
		out sp
		O2 ...
		Dx Pneumonia
		Plan Medicate as per Dr Gurdi
		Will tell
		Husband came & talk so
		we about Discontinue DNR
		Status as see wants
		everything to be done
		so I d/c DNR

DRUG ALLERGIES

it says so to discontinue DNR

Patient Identification

70411481   30-94-86
             075 Y F

10/07/2009
MEDICARE
BLUE_CBOSS

NS-14 MRC-29
FORMS 6/00, REVIEWED 3/09

DIC
ZYPREXA

PHYSICIAN'S ORDERS

(16)

Instructions: 1. Imprint patient's name before placing chart.
2. Scan to Pharmacy

☐ STAT

DATE & TIME	INITIALS & TIME	PHYSICIAN'S ORDERS AND SIGNATURES - USE BALL POINT PEN
10·13·09	0915	① 1:1 continuous observation T.O.
10·13·09	0915	② consult Katherine Rock re wound management (speed) bed. T.O. M 10/14/09 1408 10/13/09 (nd)
10·13·09	12¹⁵	EHOB cushion & boots. VO. DR BM 10/13/09 1244 10·13·09 1435 order M9
13·09·09 1545		D/C Zyprexa

SCANNED
Name:
Circle one: HUC GN LPN GN
Date & Time: 10/14/09 604

10·13·09 1640 order

Chart 6/17/6
2400

DRUG ALLERGIES

Patient Identification

70431481   30-94-56
                075 Y F

10/07/20...
MEDICARE
BLUE CROSS

1PO

PO-9 (1PO) MRC-723, FORMS 3/94 REVIEWED 4/09

- 151 -

D/C
ZYPREXA

PHYSICIAN'S ORDERS

(17)

☐ STAT

NOTE:
AUTHORIZATION IS HEREBY GIVEN TO
DISPENSE THE GENERIC OR CHEMICAL
EQUIVALENT UNLESS SPECIFICALLY
CIRCLED BY THE PHYSICIAN.

Instructions: 1. Imprint patient's name before placing in chart.
2. Fax to Pharmacy

DATE & TIME	NURSE'S INITIALS & TIME	PHYSICIAN'S ORDERS AND SIGNATURE – USE BALL POINT PEN
10/15/09	1224	Straight cath consult ← pneumonia T.O.
10/15/09 1241		
10/15/09 1302		D/C zyprexa keep foley catheter in T.O.
10/15/09 1314		continue 1:1 observation D/C ← consult consult ← pneumonia 10/15/09 1314 T.O.
10/15/09 1322		
		SCANNED Name: Circle one: HUC G LPN LN Date & Time: 10/15/09 1446
		10/15/09 1453

10/15/09
D/C
ZYPREXA

DRUG ALLERGIES

Patient Identification

70431481   30-94-58
                  075 Y F

MEDICARE
BLUE CROSS

PO-9 MRC-723 FORMS 7/04 REVIEWED 4/09

- 152 -

(handwritten: DISCHARGE LIES)

DISCHARGE SUMMARY

NAME: MR#: 30-94-56
ADMIT DATE: 10/07/2009   SEX: F DOB/AGE: 12/04/1933 75
DISCH DATE: 10/26/2009   ACCT#: 70431481
ATTENDING: M.D. (Faxed)   SS#:

        is a 75-year-old woman admitted by Dr.   on October 7th basically for comfort care and possible placement. *(handwritten: LIE)*

Hospital course was significant for patient's condition got a little bit worse with mental status changes. Her husband changed his mind from DNR/DNI to full code status. She developed CVA in the hospital and also developed pneumonia requiring intubation and followed by PEG tube placement. When I saw her today, she is still quite obtunded but she has a PEG tube and she needs oxygen. She is being placed to the   for further *(handwritten: LIE)* rehab and further management. This was discussed at length with the husband who still wants everything to be done.

DISCHARGE DIAGNOSIS
  1. CVA.
  2. Pneumonia.
  3. Dementia.

(handwritten: I ALWAYS WILL WANT EVERYTHING DONE)

(handwritten: LIE HE NEVER TALKED TO THEM)

DISCHARGE PLANNING:
She will go to   She'll get PEG tube feeding there and physical therapy as needed their.

She'll continue same medication, which she's getting here that is:
  1. XenoDerm ointment.
  2. Tylenol as needed.
  3. Nexium as needed.

(handwritten: LIE— NEVER HAD IT)

UID/lg
D: 10/26/2009 12:42   973732
T: 10/26/2009 13:11

                          M.D. (Faxed)

Authenticated by   M.D. On 10/26/2009 04:40:53 PM

Instructions: 1. Imprint patient's name before placing in chart.
2. Scan to Pharmacy

NOTE:
AUTHORIZATION IS HEREBY GIVEN TO
DISPENSE THE GENERIC OR CHEMICAL
EQUIVALENT UNLESS SPECIFICALLY
CIRCLED BY THE PHYSICIAN.

MEDS D
THE FIRST
DAY

DATE & TIME	NURSE'S INITIALS & TIME	PHYSICIAN'S ORDERS AND SIGNATURE – USE BALL POINT PEN
10/7/09 1440		IIA Urine C+S
		Dc Haldol 1mg IM Q4° PRN
		Zyprexa 2.5mg PO at H00 NOW
		Zyprexa Zydis 5mg PO HS
		Zyprexa 5mg IM Q4° PRN severe agitation

Name:
Circle one:
Date & Time   10/7/09

THEY STARTED
MY WIFE ON HALDOL

AND THEN

CALLS HGS OF

ZYPREXA
HOW MUCH IN
ONE DAY?
THEY MUST HAVE
WANTED HER
DEAD THE FIRST
DAY THERE

10/7/09

DRUG ALLERGIES

MR-013 (NS-85)
FORMS 8/01
REVIEWED 5/02

PLANS TO TAKE HER HOME SQUASH!

(20)

DATE	TIME	
10/12/09	1130	neuro

Pt's husband at bedside.
Has changed his mind about
placement to SNF. Plan is
for him to take her
home ~~w/out~~ home
health assistance.

Ø new findings. Pt sleeping.

A/L Advanced Dementia

Ø new neuro
RN

labs/test reviewed

MY PLAN CHANGED! TO TAKE HER HOME w/ HHC ASSISTANCE

DRUG ALLERGIES

NS-14 MRC-29
FORMS 6/00, REVIEWED 3/09

Case Management Information Sharing Request

Date: 10/21/09   Time: 14:30

Patient Identification

30-94-56
075 Y F

MEDICARE
BLUE CROSS

Requestor: _____   call back #: _____

☑	Call made to extension	☒	Faxing Completed (*for Medical Records*)
☐	Form put on chart/Faxed (5328)	☒	Date/Initials (*for Medical Records*)
			10/2/09

PLEASE FAX THE FOLLOWING STANDARD CHART ABSTRACT

Note: The check off blocks is for *Medical Records* use only.

☒ Front Sheet	☒ Abnormal lab cultures (All MDROs)
☒ H & P	☐ Therapy Notes (2 days) including respiratory
☒ Progress Notes (1 day)	☒ Nurses Note (1 day)
☒ Evaluations (therapy)	☒ MARS (7 days)
☐ First Page of Admission History	☐ Height & Weight

ADDITIONAL INFORMATION NEEDED TO BE FAXED (that is not listed above):

OCT 26, TO NURSING HOME
OF THE ANGELS

OTHER FACILITIES TO BE FAXED TO (not listed on back):

Pilot

Please call us immediately if the fax you receive is incomplete or illegible.

The information contained in this fax transmittal is confidential and intended only for the designated recipient. If you have received this in error you are hereby notified that review, dissemination, distribution, or copying of this information is forbidden. If this fax has been received in error, the sender should be notified immediately by telephone and the original fax returned to the sender or destroyed.

IS-59F MRC-917 FORMS 3/08